# AN INTRODUCTION TO
# CHRISTIAN FEMINISM

*Claire Colette Murphy* SHCJ

# An Introduction to
# Christian Feminism

DOMINICAN PUBLICATIONS

First published (1994) by
Dominican Publications
42 Parnell Square
Dublin 1

ISBN 1-871552-42-7

Cover design by
David Cooke.
Symbol based on an eleventh century carving
on a doorway at Manglisi Cathedral, Georgia.

Origination by
Dominican Publications.

Printed in Ireland by
Colour Books Ltd, Baldoyle, Dublin 13.

# Contents

# ONE

# Starting Point

I first met the word 'feminism' in Nigeria back in the early 1970s. I had travelled down to Calabar and there met some past-pupils who were studying at the university. They had with them the latest copy of *Time* magazine and were discussing an article on the activities of feminists in the U.S.A.

Looking at me one girl said; 'You certainly need feminism in your country. We hear that in Ireland wives have no money of their own and have to ask their husbands for everything they need.' 'Yes,' said another, 'married women have to stay in a house all day minding their children, and have no adult to talk to.' The extended family system in Africa ensures that women have plenty of adult company and shared child-minding. And just as the Irish farming wife had, in the past, her own 'hen money' so most women in this area of Nigeria had their measure of financial independence.

The fact that these young Nigerian girls regarded Irish housewives with such pity came as quite a shock. However, I thought no more about it. Nor did I consider the circumstances of the Irish mother in the home until many years later, when the Christian Feminist Movement began to investigate ways in which mothers could become financially independent. This investigation is still going on.

Cornelia Connelly was asked in 1846 to found the Society of the Holy Child Jesus, to which I belong, for the 'Catholic instruction and education of all classes'. By 1983, after twelve years of renewal in the religious life mandated by Vatican II, our new approved rules stated that we were to work for 'Christian principles of justice, peace and compassion'. This was spelled out to include 'work for wider recognition of the dignity of women', and to 'encourage fuller pastoral ministries for women in the Church'. In 1984, when I was retraining for adult education, each student had to choose an area of social concern for 'field work'. None of the students wanted to go near women's groups. So, remembering our renewed Rule, and as an good Holy Child Sister, I volunteered to study women's issues. I am stressing this point, as occasionally I am asked by women new to Christian feminism, 'Will you be allowed to stay in your Order if you talk like this?'

Little did I realise as I set out that first morning for Kilbarrack, on the north side of Dublin, and the women's educational project called 'Klear', that I was beginning a journey that would lead me into a much clearer understanding of Jesus and his mission.

Over the next few years my feminist education continued, first in a group called 'Women for Change', where we discussed books and shared experiences, then in 'Sophia', a Christian feminist group. In 1987 the Third International

Interdisciplinary Congress of Women was held in Dublin, and after it there was a felt need among some women for a new feminist voice in Ireland. As a result of net-working with women's groups around the country the Christian Feminist Movement – Ireland got started. Through its Newsletter and conferences I continued to have my awareness raised. Meanwhile, still in 1987, *Womanspirit* was launched. It appears three times a year and describes itself as 'a resource for those interested in feminist spirituality'.

At home, books on Christian feminism began to appear in the convent library and names such as Elisabeth Schüssler-Fiorenza, Marina Warner, Anne Carr, Sara Maitland, Maria O'Riley, Elizabeth Moltmann, Joan Chittister, Carolyn Osiek, Elizabeth Johnson, Sandra Schneiders, Rosemary Radford Reuther, Ursula King and Susanne Heine became known. Many of these books are highly academic and written in professional language, which for a lay reader is unfamiliar and so difficult to follow with ease.

Hence this book. It aims to give a brief overview of some Christian feminist insights. These I have gained from studying the scholars, listening to them lecture, sharing with women and men, and reflecting on the Scriptures.

**Clarifications**
Before beginning a study of *Christian* feminism it is necessary to come to a mutual understanding of terms commonly used by feminists.

Just as a fish is not aware that it lives in water, is confined by water, so women and men are often unaware that they live within, are confined by a culture. That is, by values, practices, prejudices learned in childhood and presumed to be natural, normal, the God-given way to live life.

*Patriarchy* is an all-pervasive set of attitudes that has dominated human beings for thousands of years. According to partriarchy, the male of the human species is the norm for humanity, the female is secondary, created for his service. Patriarchy has institutionalised patterns of power to control and exclude those it wishes to keep subservient. Relationships are hierarchical, authority is imposed, conflict is resolved by conquest. God is imaged as beyond, all-powerful, all-knowing, in charge, judging, controlling all things.

It is important to realise that our history, philosophy and religious understanding all express men's experience of life. Women's experiences and insights have been ignored by patriarchal culture.

*Feminism* presents an alternative understanding of life coming from the experiences and insights of women. It sees partriarchy as inhibiting the full potential of human beings, women and men. Feminism is an emerging world view that questions patriarchal attitudes, and envisions a future in which relationships of domination/submission become ones of mutuality. Feminism promotes cooperation, interdependence, consensus, and images God within the person and the community as the all-empowering Spirit.

Feminists are not anti-men but pro-human. President Mary Robinson, in a 1993 television interview, stressed the fact that feminists are not trying to feminise the world but to humanise it.

The Brazilian educationalist Paolo Freire stated that where there is a situation of oppressor and oppressed both are dehumanised but that the oppressor becomes more dehumanised than the oppressed. Therefore the oppressed has to strive to humanise both. This must be done by awareness-raising and persuasion, not by violence which would only mean continuing to behave in the patriarchal mode. Feminism is not about raising women up to the level of men, but about liberating women and men from oppressive structures and attitudes.

*Gender* is regarded by feminists as a social arrangement within patriarchy whereby roles are allocated according to a person's sex thus discounting the individual's gifts and abilities. Feminists recognise sex as biological, but do not accept that gender roles are dictated by nature, as investigation shows that they are culturally based. For example, farming in the West is considered man's work. Women farmers make headlines. Yet throughout the rest of the world the cultivation of the land is considered woman's work. It only becomes man's work when machinery is introduced.

*Masculine* and *feminine* are terms that feminists regard with suspicion. They see them as arbitrarily attributing different qualities exclusively to men or to women. Woman's experience tells her that she does not have the monopoly on gentleness, honesty, vulnerability or stupidity. Nor are all men by nature aggressive, cunning, strong and intelligent.

A mother aggressively attacking a baby-snatcher is not behaving like a man but like a woman protecting her child. A man gently nursing a sick parent is not behaving like a woman but like a caring, concerned son.

The norm, that which has become the normal, is not necessarily the natural. It is not nature that dictates women should cook and that men should govern. We have been conditioned to accept as natural what has become the norm – the gender roles allocated by our patriarchal culture.

## Feminism exists because sexism exists

It is a profound sin to label women as the source of evil in the world, as intellectually inferior, psychologically unstable and inclined to sensuality. Yet sexism does just that (U.S. Bishops, *Partners in the Mystery of Redemption*, 1988).

The feminist movement is ... one of the most significant movements in our time. In the phrase used by the Vatican Council, it must be seen as one of the 'signs of our times' which the Church must read in our age. Indeed the equality of the sexes is basic Christian teaching. Feminism can be said to have received its first charter from St Paul when he said (Gal 3:27-28): 'There are no more distinctions ... between male and female, but you are all one in Christ Jesus' (Irish Bishops, 1985).

To conclude this section we can recall again that, when speaking of feminism and patriarchy, we are speaking of two different attitudes to life coming from the separate conditioning women and men receive in childhood. For centuries man's perceptions have dominated. Today we have wars on every continent as nations try to resolve their differences. The balanced ecology of our planet is being heedlessly attacked and destroyed. Profit is valued more than people in our market places. Institutionalised religion ceased to be a counter-sign in the world when it took in the values and structures of our patriarchal society.

In the twentieth century the feminist view point has begun to emerge again and slowly we see a gathering of peoples anxious to heal old wounds and to work towards establishing more cooperative structures. We have The United Nations, the European Union, the Green Movement, the World Council of Churches, the network of the Women's Movement, to mention but a few.

The lists on page 8 give a flavour of the two different approaches.

| PATRIARCHAL | FEMINIST |
| --- | --- |
| God placed men over women and the earth | God created women and men equal and gave both responsibility for the earth (Gen 1:26) |
| Controlled from above | Animation from within |
| Authority imposed | Authority for service |
| Sees outsiders as threat | Sees potential for new friendships |
| Suppresses feelings | Trusts feelings |
| Conquest resolves conflict | Consensus resolves conflict |
| People are functional | People are unique |
| Relationships are hierarchical | Relationships are mutual |
| Insists on conformity | Encourages pluriformity |
| Achievement through competition | Achievements through co-operation |
| Tradition based | Future-oriented |
| Money is absolute | Money is symbolic |
| Subdue the earth | Nurture the earth |
| God is all-powerful. | God is all-empowering. |

Again we need to remember that feminists are not trying to feminise the world but to humanise it. That means, the insights of women and of men are necessary if we are to reach our full potential as humans: 'The glory of God is the person fully alive' (St Irenaeus, 130-200 A.D.).

REFLECTIVE PAUSE

1. List what you consider the three most important ideas expressed so far.
2. Mention one idea with which you disagree.
3. List words that express the popular understanding of feminine and masculine qualities.
4. How close are they to reality? Do the same words appear on both lists.

# TWO

# Strands of Feminism

**Religious feminists**

By the mid-twentieth century many women, inspired by the insights of feminists in the secular world, became aware that all was not well, not life-giving, within their own religions. These women believed that both feminist values and religious expression were essential for full human living.

So within the main world religions such as Hinduism, Judaism, Christianity and Islam feminist reform movements were initiated. These religious feminists differed from their secular sisters in that they were concerned with theology and the God/human relationship.

As the women in the various Christian Churches studied the Bible in the new light of feminist insights, they saw that Jesus had preached against patriarchal values and had warned his followers not to be guided by them.

However, some baptised feminists came to the conclusion that Christianity was so riddled with patriarchal values that it no longer held any Good News for them. In fact they believed the widespread influence of Christianity had undermined the dignity of women. While they continue to acknowledge the significance of the Christian culture in their own lives, they now seek spiritual nourishment in feminist spirituality.

The word 'spirituality' has been redefined over and over again. St Paul used the word to mean activity characterised by the presence of the Spirit among us. In medieval Christendom it became restricted to the lives of monks and mystics. In later centuries it was recognised as the way of relating to the sacred. Feminist spirituality encourages women to become open to the activity of the Spirit within them so that they may be transformed and become agents of transformation for others.

These feminists learned to distinguish between religion, Church, theology, spirituality, liturgy and ritual. They set out to find God in their own experiences and through developing new rituals which express their understanding of their relationship with God. They are anxious to explore the meaning of the Divine in female terms and so study ancient religions, such as the Celtic, that were comfortable with portraying the Divine as Goddess.

Some post-Christian feminists question the wisdom of imaging the Divine as female, pointing out that Goddess worship arose out of the fertility cults. They remember the time when in Christianity only women who became consecrated virgins were considered capable of a spiritual life. Other religious feminists find that worshipping the Divine as Goddess completes them as women.

## Christian feminists

Christian feminists are women and men who are committed

to the Church but who acknowledge that the Good News preached by Jesus has at times been distorted throughout the centuries of institutionalised Christianity. They are concerned not just with equality for women and justice for all, but also with the very purpose and mission of the Church. Unlike the post-Christians they believe the Church is capable of freeing itself from the secular influences of patriarchy, and of becoming a clearer imaging of the vision Jesus had for his community of believers.

When we come later to look at Jesus, we will see that by his words and actions he lived as a counter-sign to patriarchy. We will also see that he related to women in exactly the same way as he related to men.

Before we come to the section focusing on Jesus as presented in the Gospels, it will be helpful first to take time to continue to look at the various strands of feminism so as to prevent confusion and misunderstandings. Each strand has its own history and aims, and while they all strive to achieve greater harmony and justice among people, the means they take differ.

## Secular feminists

The eighteenth century European movement known as the Enlightenment provided the conditions necessary for the germination of the modern phase of feminism. The Enlightenment was based on faith in humankind. Reason was the only acceptable authority. Inspired by the new questioning women began to ask why one sex always benefitted at the expense of the other. In 1789 Olympe de Gouge wrote her Declaration of the Rights of Women. Later she was guillotined as a counter-revolutionary.

## The moral feminists

These are sometimes called the Cultural, or the Romantic feminists and their movement arose in the nineteenth century when Britain experienced the full horrors of the Industrial Revolution as rural families moved to towns in search of work.

At the same time middle class women, especially Quakers, began to organise Bible study groups. These women believed in the priesthood of all believers and, despite gender roles, were aware that women and men shared equally in the gifts of the Spirit. For them, salvation implied justice for all, women and men. However, they concluded that women were morally superior to men and so had an obligation to become involved in public life. They judged men to be aggressive, competitive, rationalistic and hard-hearted. Women they considered harmonious, creative, compassionate and holistic. They renounced patriarchy and reversed its images declaring women to be the more worthy sex.

The goals the Moral Feminists set themselves were: to end child labour, to protect women from being sold into brothels, and to secure social welfare for widows and orphans.

During that century children from the age of four worked

in mines and factories. Motherhood was valued as a source of cheap labour. By mid-century an Act of Parliament was passed raising the working age for children to nine years.

1830 saw the last record of a husband selling his wife to a brothel so as to clear his drinking debts. With a Bible in one hand and a hatchet in the other the Moral Feminists entered the bars of England preaching the Temperance Crusade. If persuasion failed to convince they used their hatchets to break open the beer barrels.

Between 1864 and 1869 the Contagious Diseases Acts were passed. In order to protect men, women in brothels were treated like public vessels and checked regularly. Patriarchy's double-standard condoned sin in men while condemning it in women.

For challenging the economic interests of men the Moral Feminists were scorned and ostracised by many Christians. Despite antagonism, these women clung to their belief that as Christians they should follow the example set by Jesus and befriend the outcasts of society.

## Liberal feminists

In 1869 John Stuart Mill wrote his book *On the Subjection of Women*. To enable women play their part in public life he sought to change the law so that women could vote and own property after marriage.

Liberal feminists declared that what defined a human was reason, and that women and men were equally rational.

Therefore, they demanded access to higher education. Their aim was to be accepted as equal citizens with equal rights before the law.

Liberal feminists did not challenge the male-centred structures of society; instead their goal was to enter them on an equal footing. To achieve this they resorted to traditional tactics of lobbying, campaigning, letter writing, and taking out legal suits. After World War I, women's agitation produced results. Between 1918 and 1920 women were given the vote in Britain and Ireland, Germany, Austria, the Netherlands, Poland, U.S.A., and the then U.S.S.R. By 1925 women in Britain were admitted to jury and magistrate service, to parliament, to universities, and to equal guardianship of their children, plus maintenance after divorce.

Liberal feminism is a revisioning of Liberal doctrine formulated by men for white male landowners. Liberal feminists did not question the structures of patriarchy or capitalism.

**Socialist feminists**

In 1826 William Thompson published his *Appeal to One Half of the Human Race*. He went beyond the Liberal struggle for legal and educational rights for women by questioning power relationships between man and woman, capitalist and worker, parent and child.

The Socialist feminists believed that the Liberal feminists' agenda would only benefit a minority of women. What was the use, they asked, of having equal rights to education and before the law, if you had no money to pay the required fees? Their goal was to achieve economic independence for women.

In an agricultural society women are part of the economic unit of the family. With the Industrial Revolution the work place was separated from the home. The concept of a 'family wage' was introduced which resulted in the wife being officially registered as an 'adult dependent' of her husband. So men were assigned to the public sphere and production while women were assigned to the private sphere and repro- duction. But the problem for women was that neither patriar- chy nor capitalism regarded 'woman's work', 'woman's proper role', or 'woman IN labour' as wage-worthy.

The nuclear family of husband, wife and children emerged under capitalism. It has been legitimised by Church authori- ties as the natural grouping, yet biblical families are extended families. Abuse within the nuclear family came to be placed beyond the law. Socialist feminists decided that the depend- ent role of women in the nuclear family was a contributing cause to the domination of men over women. They became more convinced than ever that the economic independence of women was essential, especially for women caught in a violent situation. These feminists highlighted the poverty of dependent wives which became all too evident when women were separated or divorced.

However, women are not just economically oppressed. A fulfilled and happy housewife proves that marriage is more than economic dependence. Therefore, Socialist feminists looked also to relationships. They encouraged shared parenting and asked for the definition of family to extend to a wider network of relationships. They also promoted the idea of the child as a full citizen and not the private property of the parents.

Socialism believed that the narrow concept of family was the source of private property and self-interest, that the family was the place in which such values were passed on. They saw that actions taken for the betterment of one's own family were considered praiseworthy, justified, even though in reality they were harmful to the wider community. For example, a factory owner who in time of recession sold off a section of his factory in order to finance his children's education, went unchallenged, even though some of his workers and their children were left destitute.

Social feminism is a reinterpreting of Marxist thought which was written by men from men's experiences. Social feminists challenge the Socialists to examine their patriarchal structures. They seek to humanise the workplace and ask for flexitime, job-sharing, and more part-time jobs to be made the norm.

Socialist feminists do not believe the few can change society; so they are concerned about any issue that divides women into separate categories such as coloured women, working women, housewives, each competing against the other. They accuse Church, school and family of promoting class strata, and they see these institutions as included in their struggle to end sexism, the evil of racism and classism as well. Many women believe socialism is essential to feminism, as it keeps issues of concern to all who are discriminated against by patriarchy, firmly on the public agenda.

## Radical feminists

Radical feminism appeared first in the United States where it grew out of the Civil Rights Movement in the 1960s. In 1963 Betty Friedan produced *The Feminine Mystique*. She focused on housewives and aimed to liberate those among them who felt frustrated because they believed their full potential was stifled. Like the Liberal feminists she refrained from questioning the patriarchal system as such; instead she hoped to win for women a better role in it. The sexual issues concerning women, such as rape, incest, prostitution, lesbianism and abortion she left unexamined.

In 1963 the American public had had their level of consciousness sufficiently raised to allow the acceptance of the Equal Pay Act. Ten years later, the Women's Liberation Movement succeeded in getting The Equal Pay Act passed in Britain. They used the same tactics as the students. Demonstrations and marches replaced political and legal lobbying. They campaigned against beauty competitions and the use of women as sex objects. Sisterhood was promoted. They excluded men since they believed the men's interest in the women's ideas would soon shift to their bodies. Men, they saw, were automatically allowed to fill the leading roles in other groups, and they felt it was necessary to provide women with their own safe space in which to develop their own voice and learn leadership skills.

These first Radical feminists were mainly middle-class women who had benefitted from the earlier struggles of the Liberal feminists. They became acutely aware that their Liberal mothers and aunts had not got to the root of patriarchal domination. They saw that injustice against women went deeper than politics, law or economics but was to be found rooted in culture. They rejected the idea that anatomy is destiny. A person, they said, was born female but had to learn to become a woman, because our ideas of womanhood and manhood are socially constructed and expressed in gender roles. Our patriarchal culture sees man as the norm for humanity and defines woman as functional in relation to him.

Radical feminists studied gender stereotypes and found that patriarchal values were dominant in Church, politics, industry, universities, medicine, home and bedroom. In all areas of society women were there to service men.

These Radical women decided to resist stereotyping and so showed their anger openly. They talked of separatism, of female communities and relationships. During this first stage the Radical feminists were seen as aggressive, man-hating women who undermined the dignity of the 'woman in the home'. In the public mind the Radicals represented all feminists.

By the second stage of development the Radical feminists have become more inclusive and holistic. They aim to achieve mutuality between men and women, to free women and men from gender roles and allow each to be treated according to their giftedness, and to bring an end to women being regarded as functions or property. They work through small non-leadership groups promoting a more woman-centred culture. In 1980 Adrienne Rich pointed out that the word 'revolution' means returning to the same spot. She cautions that the revolving door of feminism will be tolerated by patriarchy only within a confined space.

The Radical feminists were the only branch of feminism to have concerned themselves with religion. They saw religion as legitimising woman's subordinate role and, at the same time, as offering a potential source of empowerment for the liberation of women.

## Differing attitudes among women

The four strands of secular feminism we've been discussing show that there is no such thing as a worldwide global sisterhood. Rather, feminism is often referred to as a rainbow sisterhood. Women's experiences differ and cannot be universalised. Occasionally you will hear a feminist generalise about women. 'Women like to work in informal groups.' 'Women prefer to worship with the whole body.' Such statements come from within the speaker's own experiences and perceptions. Some women need the freedom from group pressure that structures provide. Other women prefer to worship in silent contemplation. Afro-American women have accused feminists of speaking out of their privileged white experience. While white American women were lobbying for access to the work-place, their Afro-American sisters were longing to be free of their menial jobs so as to spend more time caring for their children.

In 1979 Betty Friedan promoted the family as a safe haven from the impersonal world of patriarchal institutions. Socialist feminists accused her of an ostrich mentality. The disagreements between women are many.

ON WAR   Liberal feminists, believing in equal access for women and men, would agree to the drafting of women into the armed forces. Moral and Radical feminists condemn war and see it as a patriarchal invention in which women should have no part. They would like to see the theory that 'might is right' rejected by men altogether.

ON ECONOMICS   Liberal feminists seek to move women up the ladder. Socialist feminists strive to transform the structures so as to achieve a more equal distribution of resources.

ON MATERNITY LEAVE   Moral feminists seek laws to provide mothers with paid time with their infants. This they see as a just means of counterbalancing the obligations nature places on women. Liberal feminists see such a law as discriminating against men. Fearing such a law would prevent women securing full-time careers, they question the advantage of such a law. Socialist feminists would lobby for both maternity and paternity leave.

ON PORNOGRAPHY   Radical feminists would seek to have it outlawed. Liberal feminists would regard such a ban as against freedom of expression.

ON ABORTION   A great many feminists are anti-abortion. Being anti-abortion does not imply being anti-feminist. But some feminists make abortion on demand their goal.

Despite the many differences of opinion among feminists all are united in their effort to have women and men treated as equal, and to free both sexes from gender roles for which they are not by nature gifted. Not all women are good at parenting, not all men can cope with the role of sole 'bread-winner'.

## Conservatice women

There are many women who do not experience themselves as oppressed. They see themselves as complementing men and are proud of their role in contributing to a stable community and family life. These women have the support of the Churches, but also of the fundamentalists and right-wing groups.

Feminists see these women as colonised and used by the Establishment. Conservative women see feminists as causing stress in families, and judge the poverty of women to be caused by the breakdown in family life. Feminists attribute it to the inequalities in the work-place. Conservative women often say, 'I'm not a feminist but … '. When they do hold the same values as feminists they call them 'feminine values' – anti-violence, or pro-care for the disadvantage. They remain firmly aloof from the feminist movement. Feminists need to be open to criticism made by conservative women and to seek dialogue with them.

Feminism, as you must now realise, has a rich diversity of histories, ideologies and insights. It is important to recognise the differences and allow each strand follow its own agenda. As issues of common interest arise the various strands come together and support each other.

REFLECTIVE PAUSE

1. List aspects of the various strands of feminism with which you feel comfortable.
2. In one sentence, express your reaction to the fact that feminism contains a rainbow of ideas and does not speak with one voice.

THREE

# Jesus and Patriarchy

Jesus spent his public life proclaiming the Kingdom of God. For the Jews this term held the hope of a return to political and material fulfilment. They longed for the day when the Romans would leave their land; then peace and justice would prevail as they were ruled by their own leaders in their own land. Surely then their pagan neighbours would realise that Yahweh was the only God.

The Kingdom Jesus preached was not confined to any specific place or time. The values of God's Kingdom as taught by Jesus were often the very opposite of the patriarchal values accepted in the society of his day. The cultural traditions, the authority structures, the customs, taboos and prejudices of this society, whether religious or secular, he questioned persistently. He called for inner conversion and modelled new ways of relating to people.

## The exercise of authority
At the end of the Sermon on the Mount, Matthew records (7:28-29) that the people where amazed because Jesus taught, not like the teachers of the Law, but as one who had authority. For Jesus, authority meant service given for the well-being of

others. It was a service exercised without fear and with inner certainty, unlike patriarchal authority which depended on hierarchy and the opportunity to dominate and control others. Jesus invited people to listen, to hear, then left them free to respond as they wished; of his disciples he asked if they too wanted to go as had those who could not accept his teachings (John 6:67).

Jesus lived and died an orthodox Jew. He attended syna- gogue each Sabbath and travelled south to the temple in Jerusalem for the annual festivals. He paid his temple tax (Matthew 17:24) and sent lepers to the priest to be certified clean 'according to the law of Moses'. Yet he felt free to question rules and to set them aside at times. Right at the beginning of his Gospel Mark records an incident in which religious leaders accused the disciples of breaking the Sab- bath law. They had picked and eaten some grain because they were hungry. Jesus defended them saying that the Sabbath was instituted to serve the people, not to be served by the people (2:27).

Towards the end of his life Jesus accused the religious leaders of emphasising externals and neglecting the impor- tant teachings on justice, mercy and honesty. He called them blind leaders who strain a fly out of a cup but swallow a camel (Matthew 22:23-24).

He accused them of introducing to their own benefit teachings contrary to the law of God, and referred to *corban* whereby money needed for the care of parents, if donated to the temple, excused a son of his filial obligations (Matthew 7:9-13).

When the men exercising religious authority flaunted the secular trappings of patriarchy Jesus was forthright in his condemnation of their acquired titles, their distinctive dress and special seats in the synagogue (Matthew 23:1-12). He reminded his disciples that among the pagans their rulers made their authority felt and asked them not to let that happen in their community (Matthew 20:23-26). On his last night with the disciples Jesus knelt down and washed their feet; rising he asked them to do likewise and gave them a new commandment, to love (John 13:1-15; 15:12).

## Equality *versus* status

At around thirty years of age Jesus gave up his carpentry and became an itinerant teacher. The Gospels record Jesus in lively debate with the rabbis and teaching in the porches of the temple. He never identified with the priestly caste; instead he associated himself with the prophet John who preached a social morality and administered a baptism of conversion down by the Jordan. John asked his followers to live justly: if soldiers, not to abuse their power; if tax collectors, not to overcharge; if propertied, to share their food and clothing with those who had less (Luke 3:10-21).

When Jesus returned to his home town of Nazareth he attended the synagogue on the Sabbath and was given the Book of Isaiah to read and interpret. He chose the passage that described the task of the prophet – to bring good news to the poor, free the oppressed and enable the blind to see. Jesus declared this too was his role. His townspeople were outraged at his claim and tried to kill him (Luke 4:16-30).

Thus began the ministry of Jesus. From the beginning his teaching brought hope to some and a sense of foreboding to others. His teaching never changed and the week before he was killed he outlined the social morality expected of those entering God's Kingdom. They were to feed the hungry, clothe the naked, visit the sick and the prisoners, and offer shelter to the stranger (Matthew 25:34-36).

The religious people among whom Jesus lived believed that riches were a sign of God's favour, that the poor must have offended God and so deserved their sufferings. Jesus shared meals and companionship with the poor and the outcasts (Mark 2:15-17). Nor did he feel any concern about protecting his reputation in the interest of his mission. On the contrary, he sounded amused when responding to his critics: he remarked that John the Baptist fasted and they said he was possessed while he himself ate and drank and they called him a glutton and drunkard (Luke 7:33-35).

The Kingdom of God included not only the outcasts of Jewish society but was open to the Gentiles as well. People from north, south, east and west, Jesus said, would feast together in the Kingdom (Luke 13:29). Jesus was himself surprised by the Spirit-filled faith of the Gentile centurion and the Canaanite woman. Later, when pushed by a teacher of the law to say who exactly counted as neighbour, Jesus chose as an example of Kingdom behaviour the actions of a semi-pagan Samaritan. A Levite and a priest saw a stranger injured by the wayside but passed him by. The Samaritan stopped, brought the man to an inn and there cared for him (Luke 10:25-37). The community Jesus envisaged, unlike patriarchy, was all-inclusive.

The religious leaders of the time rightly saw Jesus as a threat to their traditions and privileged position. They gathered in council and Caiaphas, the high priest, declared that it was better that one man die than that their nation be undermined (John 11:50). Had Jesus preached a devotional relationship with God that did not challenge the *status quo* he would not have ended his life on a cross. Christian feminists put it this way: Jesus came on earth to live among us and because of the way he lived he died on the cross.

## Jesus and women
In the nineteenth century women brought up in the Reformed Churches were allowed to follow advanced studies in theology and scripture. Roman Catholic women had few such opportunities as these studies were in most countries confined to seminaries. With the changed outlook brought about by Vatican II in the early 1970s Catholic women could at last pursue theology and scripture to doctorate level. In the 1970s and 1980s they published their findings and brought a new sense of spiritual fulfilment to many women and some men.

Their works were of necessity highly academic so that more popular books by Christian feminists are only coming on the market in recent years. These women realised that the traditional interpretation given to Scripture passages all came from the male experience of life. They tried to come to the Bible with fresh minds interpreting the text from a woman's perspective.

As they studied the Gospels and watched Jesus in action they saw that Jesus treated women in exactly the same way he treated men. He did not romanticise or patronise women, nor did he regard their sex as the sole purpose of their being. When a woman in the crowd called out blessing the womb that bore him and the breasts he sucked, Jesus was quick to put her right stressing that rather blessed was she who studied and followed the law of God (Luke 11:27-28). Women, like men, had need of conversion, Jesus described some women as foolish and others as wise (Matthew 25:1-13).

Jesus took women seriously and accepted that, like men, they too could be intelligent, courageous and loyal. He talked with them, listened to them and responded – even the woman in the crowd was acknowledged and answered. To the disciples' surprise, he engaged in a long theological conversation with the Samaritan woman and later we find him in another deep theological exchange with Martha which shows that she had developed her spiritual knowledge as well as her catering skills (John 4 and 11).

Perhaps the most interesting encounter was with the

Canaanite woman, a Gentile, who asked Jesus to cure her daughter. Jesus answered that he had come only for the people of Israel. She challenged him to extend his ministry, saying the dogs ate the crumbs let fall at table. Jesus recognised that she spoke with the power of the Spirit, rejoiced in her faith – and what she asked was done (Matthew 15:21-28). Earlier on, it was another woman, Mary, who made it known to Jesus that the time to start his public ministry had come when she asked him to change the water into wine (John 2:4-5).

Jesus did not allow social taboos interfere with his relationship with women. He touched them (think of Peter's mother-in-law and of Jairus' daughter) and he accepted the touch of the woman who washed his feet. He made himself ritually unclean by drinking the water he had asked of the Samaritan woman, and when touched by the haemorrhaging woman he made no effort to be purified.

Women scholars noted that all four Gospels recorded the feeding of the five thousand men. This incident took place in the desert. No doubt the women were at home minding the children. Not so, according to Matthew who confirms there were five thousand men NOT COUNTING THE WOMEN AND CHILDREN (14:21). So the women were there but like the children were of no account for the records.

Whenever you see the disciples mentioned, visualise women and men, do not expect to find the women's presence recorded. Jesus accepted women disciples and they travelled with him from village to village (Luke 8:1-3). Yet nowhere are Jesus or his male followers accused by his religious critics of immoral conduct with the women. Jesus obviously expected his men followers to treat the women as co-workers in a discipleship of equals. Women were not to be regarded as objects; to lust after a woman was sinful, as lust is an act of the will (Matthew 5:28).

Nor did Jesus stereotype the sexes. A striking example of this is found in Luke 15. Here we have the well-known story of the Prodigal Son. No mother is mentioned but the father is described as displaying attitudes we have been taught to associate with women. He was passive, waiting and watching for his son's return. When finally the son was sighted the father's main emotion was pity – he rushed to hug and kiss his son and was immediately concerned with the young man's appearance; nothing would do but the best clothes and jewellery. Then he organised a welcome home feast. Compare this with a lesser known story told in the same chapter. A woman lost, not a child, but money – the source of independence and influence. She immediately asserted herself, lit a lamp and swept the house until she found it.

Switching over the stereotypes seems to have come quite naturally to Jesus. Perhaps this is not surprising seeing that in a given moment he could himself express both what we call masculine and feminine emotions. The incident occurred when Jesus was approaching Jerusalem and some rabbis warned him not to enter the city as Herod had men on the lookout to kill him. Jesus' response was pure macho as he defied them to 'go tell that fox' that he would continue to work both today and tomorrow. Then looking down on the city he became tender, comparing himself to a mother hen who protectively gathered her chicks under her wings for so he longed to care for the people, but they would not let him (Luke 13:31-34). It is sometimes asked by women why Jesus' chosen image is never used as a Christ symbol. We are familiar with the lamb and the fish, even the crowing cock is remembered in religious art, but not the mother hen.

A similar downgrading of the female is found in the records of Jesus' last week on earth. While Jesus was at table in the house of Simon in Bethany a woman entered, broke open a jar of pure nard and anointed the head of Jesus, just as Samuel had anointed the head of Saul, God's chosen one. The significance of her gesture was lost on those present as they quibbled over her wastefulness. Jesus defended her action declaring that wherever the Good News was proclaimed she would be remembered (Mark 14:3-9). The name of the man whose ear Peter cut off in Gethsemane is known but the name of this woman has gone unrecorded.

It is the growing awareness of these omissions that urges women to study anew the significance of women in the life of Jesus and the early Christian community. The importance of this study lies not in enhancing women but in learning to understand God more.

The teaching Church emphasises the sexual differences between women and men claiming that they are complementary. If so, then this is all the more reason as to why women's experiences and perceptions should be included and allowed to contribute to the Church's understanding of the faith. Being a woman is another way of being human.

When the religious authorities finally persuaded the Roman governor to arrest Jesus the women disciples continued to follow him right to Mount Calvary. They remained to see him buried and were the first back to the tomb on Easter morning intent on anointing his body. Instead they were the first to be presented with the mystery of the resurrection and were missioned by the risen Christ to bring the Good News to the brethren who regarded their words as nonsense and would not believe them. Later, Jesus rebuked the apostles for refusing to believe 'those who had seen him alive'. Years later when writing to the Corinthians Paul omits any reference to the women in his list of resurrection appearances (1 Corinthians 15:3-7). Patriarchy would not accept the witness of women.

With Jesus, women had the experience of being included, of being equal and trusted. Instead of the exclusive rite of circumcision Jesus pronounced baptism to be the initiation ritual of the Christian community. In his baptism statement Paul expressed the mind of Jesus – 'there is no difference between Jew and Gentile, slave and free, men and women, you are all one in Jesus, the Christ' (Galatians 3:28).

REFLECTIVE PAUSE

List aspects of the worldwide Christian communities that Jesus might challenge today.

FOUR

# The Churches Founded by Paul

For Paul and the communities he established, baptism was not a vertical relationship between the individual and God. On the contrary, it was a horizontal commitment empowered by Christ in which individuals became members of a community of equals and the old social divisions between them ceased.

It must have been extremely hard for a Greek or Jewish man to accept women and slaves as equals. There could be no more offering of the traditional prayers thanking God for not being a woman, a slave, a Gentile or a barbarian. For the newly converted Christian women and slaves, it must have been equally hard to behave responsibily as equals. The house-Church was the primary focus for these early Christians. After celebrating the Sabbath in the synagogue the Jewish Christians joined with the Greek converts in a local house to await in vigil the return of Jesus and to celebrate the Eucharist.

Paul's letters are our earliest Christian documents. They were written before the Gospels, between the years 50 and 60 A.D. In them, the ministry of women as co-ministers with men is taken for granted. Women were prophets, teachers and administrators. There is reference to the Church that meets in Chloe's house (1 Corinthians 1:11) and in the house of

Nympha (Colossians 4:15). Women prophesy at the assembly (1 Corinthians 11:5). Euodia and Syntyche are described as two co-workers who had a disagreement (Philippians 4:2-3). The women scholars point out that Paul used the same phrase to acknowledge the ministries of Luke, Titus and Timothy. In Romans 16, Priscilla, Mary, Typhaena, Tryphosa and Julia are co-workers who 'labour hard for the sake of the Gospel'. In the same chapter Phoebe is described as a deacon and Junia as an apostle.

It is clear that the Holy Spirit did not discriminate between women and men in the distribution of gifts: 'I will send down my Spirit upon you, and your sons and your daughters will prophesy' (Acts 2:17). The charisms of prophesy, ministry, teaching, evangelising, and leadership were not gender-based (Romans 12:6-8). Terms like 'faithful', 'believer', 'disciple', 'witness' applied equally to women and to men. Love, joy, peace, patience, kindness, goodness, faithfulness, humility and self-control were not 'feminine' virtues, but were the fruits of the Spirit to be bestowed equally on men (Galatians 5:22).

Luke in the Acts of the Apostles described the founding of Christian communities between 50 and 60 A.D. In chapter 16:11-15 we have the first record of a house-Church founded in Europe. The leader was Lydia who ran a cloth business in the Greek city of Philippi. When Paul and Silas arrived in the city they made their way on the Sabbath to 'a place of prayer' down by the riverside. There Paul met Lydia with a group of women and he sat down and instructed them. Lydia believed and was baptised with all her household. She persuaded the two missionaries to lodge in her house. Soon after, when Paul and Silas were arrested and later released, they immediately made there way to the house of Lydia where they found the believers gathered in prayer. They spoke to them words of encouragement and then the two apostles left the city. Towards the end of his life Paul wrote affectionately to the community in Philippi and thanked them for all the help they had sent him. There is no mention of Lydia but Paul in his letter was concerned about a disagreement between Euodia and Syntyche and begged the two women to make peace. He wrote of them as co-workers who had laboured with himself, Clement and others in spreading the Gospel of Christ (Philippians 4:2-3).

The woman co-worker we know most about is Priscilla, sometimes called Prisca. She, together with her husband Aquila, led house-Churches in Corinth, Ephesus and Rome. They were already Christians and settled in Corinth when Paul met them; and as all three were tent-makers they invited him to move in and live and work with them. Eighteen months later they travelled to Ephesus with Paul and presided over a house-Church there. It was here that they came across Apollos preaching the baptism of John and together they instructed him concerning faith in Jesus. Apollos accepted their teaching and became a Christian evangelist (Acts 18). The couple must have gone to Rome, for, in his Letter to the Romans, Paul sent greetings to Priscilla and Aquila and to the Church that met in their house. He referred to them as co-labourers who had risked their lives in the service of Christ (16:3-5).

## Interpreting the Bible

Though Paul never accompanied Jesus during his ministry in Palestine or saw him relate to women and out-casts, he grasped the core message of equality which was to be practised in the Christian community irrespective of race, class or sex. We have just seen that Paul accepted women in leadership roles in the Church; yet despite this fact, he has received a bad press in recent years and is considered by many to be anti-woman. Certainly, some of the letters attributed to Paul contain statements that undermine the Good News for women.

So we are faced with what look very much like contradictions within the Bible and these require some knowledgeable interpretation. Some texts in the letters of Paul and those written in his name are much clearer than others in carrying the message preached by Christ. For example, which of the following texts would you regard as closer to the attitude of Jesus: 'Wives, obey your husbands' (Ephesians 5:22), or 'Husbands, love your wives' (Ephesians 5:25)?

Texts can be found to support each side of an argument. Those who support the ministry of women in the Church quote 1 Corinthians 11:5 which asks the women who 'proclaim the message' at the assembly to cover their heads. Those who do not support the idea of women in ministry quote a text that actually appears three chapters later in the same letter, which declares that women must act according to the Jewish law – they keep quiet in church, not be in charge, and to be instructed by their husbands at home (14:34-35). The Corinthian Christians must have found the instructions concerning women very confusing. Then we find Paul contradicting his instructions to the Christians of Corinth when he wrote to the Galatians; 'Christ has set us free. If you try to please God by keeping the Jewish law, then you no longer follow Christ' (4:1.4).

What do the scholars say? Some believe that Paul had truly 'put on the mind of Christ' in his attitude to women and slaves, but with persecution hovering in the background, together with his anxiety to have Christ accepted among the Gentiles, that Paul made some tactical concessions to the surrounding cultural pressures. If true, it was something Jesus never did, he was clearly counter-cultural, and content to let people accept or reject his message. Others believe that it was Paul's disciples who succumbed to the pressures and so edited the apostle's teachings. We know the pastoral letters were written many years after Paul's death. Another theory is that as women exercised leadership roles among the Gnostics, the Marcians and other Christian groups regarded as heretical, mainstream Christianity began to suspect the influence of women. It is a chicken or egg question – Which came first? Some scholars wonder if women finding themselves marginalised later by the Pauline Churches moved to Gnostic and other groups where they saw their God-given gifts were appreciated and allowed to be exercised.

Finally, others hold that the text is original but that patriarchy has misinterpreted Paul's words. For example, let us go back to the controversial passages in 1 Corinthians 11:2-16. Here Paul asked women to grow their hair long and to cover it with a veil. What is going on here? Jesus never told women what to wear or how to style their hair. The scholars tell us Paul was not concerned with hair but with sexuality. In Corinth, apparently, homosexuals grew their hair long and lesbians cut theirs short. Earlier in the letter Paul had strongly condemned the sexual immorality of the Corinthian Christians, and maybe he was over-anxious when he urged them to conform to the conventional fashions. It is not unknown for boys in Catholic schools to have been penalised for wearing their hair long or, stranger still, for growing their beards.

The Greek word *exousia* is traditionally translated as 'veil', but we are told its basic meaning is 'authority'. Therefore, instead of Paul telling women to wear veils, some say, he was instead reaffirming their authority to teach and prophesy. It is pointed out that, in verses 11 and 12, Paul reiterates the equality and interdependence between women and men, reminding the Corinthians that if woman was made from the rib of man, man was born of woman.

Women who have come to suspect the interpretations of men, see the passage as the outpourings of a homesick Jew. Paul, they say, was used to seeing his mother and aunts veiled according to the Jewish custom, whereas Greek women went unveiled, displaying their ornately plaited hair. So this patriarchial man imposed his cultural traditions on vulnerable women, while he championed the men by defending them against the law of circumcision.

The word *diakonos* when used to describe the role of men is translated as deacon; but when Paul applied the same term to Phoebe it was translated as servant or deaconess (Romans 16:1-2). Phoebe, like Priscilla, Barnabas and Silas travelled from Church to Church in the service of Christ. It has been noted that Paul never appointed leaders, rather, he acknowledged those who on account of the service they gave were accepted by their communities (1 Thessalonians 5:12). It has also been noted that Paul never once made mention of a woman presiding at the Eucharist; neither, for that matter, does he mention a man presiding at the Eucharist.

**The second generation**
Now we come to the pastoral letters bearing Paul's name but written over forty years after his death by a second generation of Christians. Here, within the pages of Scripture, we find that a community of equals has become an authoritarian Church.

It is clear from the letters of Paul that he expected the return of Jesus during his own life-time. He advised his converts not to marry but to prepare for the coming of Christ; some even gave up work. Now those heady days were over, and those who had known Jesus in the flesh were gone. In 70A.D. the temple and its priestly caste in Jerusalem were destroyed. In Rome and throughout the empire, the persecution of Christians had increased and, through fear, the Jews expelled the Christians from their synagogues. The Church had reached the second phase of the development process, that of consolidation. It was now the duty of the leaders to set up a formal structure to ensure the passing on of the Good News, to gather the documentary evidence and to edit it.

An interesting example of editing seems to have been carried out on Romans 16:7. It has been noted already that Paul referred to the apostle Junia: 'Greetings ... to those outstanding apostles Andronicus and Junia, Jews like myself, imprisoned with me and who became Christians before me.' It is speculated that, like Priscilla, Junia was part of a ministering couple. However, the editors apparently changed the female name Junia, which appears in other documents, to Junias, a name not recorded elsewhere.

Finally, let us look at the subtle shift which, some believe, introduced the negative approach to women in the Church. In 57 A.D. Paul wrote to the Corinthians saying, 'I am afraid that you will be corrupted and will turn from the faith, just as Eve was seduced by Satan' (2 Corinthians 11:3). Note that Paul was writing to the whole Church and so compared both men and women to Eve. Fifty years later, in 110 A.D., the writer of the First Letter to Timothy declared that women were to be silent in Church and to have no authority over men, because it was not Adam who disobeyed, but the woman, Eve. Women, he added, would be saved through child-bearing (2:11-15). 'Oneness in Christ' is forgotten and woman has become the 'cause of sin'. The counter-cultural stance taken by Jesus on behalf of women is ignored. Patriarchy has reasserted itself and the long history of the diminishment of women by the Church has begun.

REFLECTIVE PAUSE

1. The communities founded by Paul accepted the ministry of women. List the attitudes to women ministering in the Church today.
2. List ways in which women discourage women today.

# FIVE

# The Early Church

Christianity started as a renewal movement within Judaism.
The Jewish Christians continued to attend synagogue and,
thirty years after the death of Jesus, the local Christian
community in Jerusalem sent Paul to have a sacrifice offered
in the Temple (Acts 21:17-27).

However, when the Romans sacked the Temple in 70 A.D.
the Jewish priesthood died out and the rabbis became the
leaders who kept the Jewish people united through the observ-
ance of the Jewish Law, the Torah.

The Christians were known to hold sacred vigils on the
Saturday night. Misunderstandings and rumours about secret
Christian rituals so abounded that the Christians became the
obvious scapegoats at times of national crisis. As spasmodic
persecution of the Christians erupted throughout the empire,
the rabbis feared for the safety of their people and expelled the
Christians from the synogogues.

It is interesting to note that in the Gospels of Mark,
Matthew and Luke those who opposed Jesus were the priests
and teachers of the Law. But in John's Gospel, written at the
end of the century well after the expulsion of the Christians
from the synogogues, the enemies of Jesus are simply called

the Jews. Within the Scriptures the seeds of anti-Semitism were sown.

There is no reason to idealise the early Church. It was full of cultural tension consisting as it did of Jews, Greeks, Romans, other Gentiles, slaves and free, rich and poor, not to mention, women and men. It struggled to proclaim the Good News despite persecution and to a society that was becoming more and more decadent. Within the Church splinter groups appeared, of which the Gnostics were the most influential.

## Gnosticism

The origins of Gnosticism are unknown. It probably existed before the time of Jesus and certainly there were Gnostics within the early Christian community. It is sometimes said that John's Gospel bears traces of their influence.

The word *Gnostic* means 'knowledge'. The Gnostics believed that redemption was achieved through a knowledge that overcame the power of darkness. They considered the body to be evil as it imprisoned the spirit, and so they preached a sexual asceticism. The statement that women were to be saved through child-bearing would have been unacceptable to them. Their attitude forced the Church to take up the position of defending sexuality. The Gnostics sometimes referred to God as *Metropator* ie. Mother-Father God, and they practised equality in ministry. They also trusted in the Spirit of God to guide and enlighten them, and so felt no need to establish authoritative structures. While Church leaders taught that the Spirit guided the Church through the authority of the bishops, the successors of the apostles, the Gnostics described the bishops as 'dry canals'.

Some scholars believe that the pastoral letters, which were written to the whole Church, were mainly concerned with warning the Christians against the influence of the Gnostic teachings: 'avoid Godless talk and what some people call "knowledge" ' (1 Timothy 6:20). The Gnostics continued as a distinct group for about five hundred years.

## Women in ministry

Many women in the early Church centred their lives within their households, dependent on their husbands and submissive to them. If married to pagans, they were exhorted to live lives of modesty and obedience and so by example to win their husbands to Christ (1 Peter 3:1). Other women, as we have seen, ran their own businesses, had dependents and exercised leadership roles. They presided over house-Churches, travelled as missionaries and, in some cases, shared a ministry with their husbands.

Despite the fact that the old patriarchal attitudes were infiltrating the Christian communities, women continued to exercise the service of leadership. Records tell of two women deacons tortured in Asia Minor, and the 'Acts of Paul' tell the story of Thecla. She was converted by the apostle and formally commissioned by him as a missionary. She spent her life in Iconium 'enlightening many with the word of God'.

Just as Jesus had no illusions about women and realised that, like men, some were faithful and others unreliable, so the records show women carrying out their ministries with differing levels of commitment. The community in Thyatira was condemned for tolerating as their teacher 'Jezebel', an immoral woman who, contrary to Church law, ate meat offered to idols (Revelation 2:18-23). The prophetesses Maximilla and Priscilla left the main Christian community and started a new sect with Montanus in 170 A.D.

In 193 A.D. Marcia was martyred. She was a concubine of the Emperor Commodus and while he lived served the Christians working in the mines, saving many from death. In the same century Blandina was hung as bait in the form of a cross, she strengthened the Christians who watched her martyrdom as they saw in her the crucified Christ.

By the beginning of the third century negative attitudes towards women had gathered force. In Carthage the bishop forbade women to teach or baptize. The women protested and in support of their ministry quoted Paul's missioning of Thecla. In an address to women, Tertullian, no doubt influenced by the Eve reference in 1 Timothy 2:11-15, wrote:

Do you not know that you are each an Eve? God's sentence on your sex lives on into this generation. Therefore, the guilt is of necessity with you still. You are the devil's gateway, you are the plunderer of the forbidden tree, you are the first to break the divine law, it was you who persuaded the man whom the devil was not brave enough to attack. You destroyed so easily man, who is the image of God; on account of you the Son of Man had to die.

Today women point out that Eve was persuaded by the strange phenomenon of a talking snake, whom she obliged to argue with her first, while Adam was persuaded by his wife.

Clement, Bishop of Alexandria, regarded women as a source of shame: 'Nothing for man is shameful, for man is endowed with reason; as for woman it is unworthy to even think about her nature.'

In 315 A.D. the persecution of Christians ended when the Emperor Constantine legalised their communities. He bestowed on their presbyters the same privileges enjoyed by the pagan Roman priesthood. They were exempted from military service and given special roles at State festivals. And so, slowly but surely, the renewal movement initiated by Jesus became institutionalised and a community of equals became a two-tiered Church divided into two states, the clerical and the lay.

Throughout these developments women continued to minister in some of the Churches. Romana and Publia served as deacons in Antioch. In Constantinople, Bishop Nectarius ordained as deacon Olypius, a twenty-six year old widow. The year was 393 A.D. The following century Hilaria, the daughter of Remy, Bishop of Rheims, was ordained a deacon.

The following prayer appears in the Rite of Ordination for Deacons, found in the *Rituale Graecorum* of Venice:

O Lord, grant the grace of the most Holy Spirit to this servant of yours who offers herself to you for ministry. Give her this grace just as the grace of the diaconate was given to Phoebe to enable her to carry out her ministry.

Even while such women were carrying out their ordained ministries in various areas of the Church John Chrysostom wrote: 'The presbyter should in his concern for men, not forget the needs of women, who require greater pastoral care because of their inclination to sin.' And again, 'Women are weak and frivolous. Their surest hope for salvation lies in their bearing children.' This was written three hundred years after the letter to Timothy. Five years after the ordination of Olypius, Chrysostom became Patriarch of Constantinople: he died in 407 A.D.

Augustine, later declared a Doctor of the Church, was a contempory of John Chrysostom. Among his writings appear these two statements: 'According to the natural order, women are destined to be subject to men, and children to their parents, for it is only just that the weaker reason be controlled by the stronger.' And: 'When a woman is considered as the helpmate of man, which is the state that belongs to her, she is not the image of God. Rather the man is the image of God solely by his nature, which is so whole that it makes a perfect image, and a woman when joined to him becomes part of this one image.'

## Patriarchy in the Church

When in the early 1960s John XXIII called Vatican II, he

asked us to return to our roots, that is, to the Gospels. It is important to realise that the Christian Bible not only records the teachings and acts of Jesus, but also the accommodation the early Church made to patriarchy as the religious leaders gradually adopted some of the structures, the ceremonials, and the attitudes of the surrounding secular society.

There is no useful reason for labouring the negative patriarchial attitudes to women, except to stress that their influence still permeates the Church at the end of the twentieth century. So just two quotes will suffice to bridge the intervening centuries: 'Woman was made to be a help to man. But she is only fit for procreation, as another man would prove a more useful helpmate in anything else' (Thomas Aquinas, thirteenth century). And 'God has done a great favour for man in giving him woman, both for procreation and the containment of lust' (Martin Luther, sixteenth century).

It may be argued that both Tertullian and Luther left the mainstream Christianity of their day and so are not representative. But these attitudes are still found today in papal documents which refer to women only as 'wives' and 'mothers', thus defining them by their biological functions in relation to men. Often women are described as 'adult dependents' and so are relegated to the same status as their children in their relationship to their husbands.

The *Catholic Children's Bible* , on sale in Church-owned bookshops, paraphrased Genesis 2:21-22 as follows: 'The Lord God then cast Adam into a deep sleep, and from Adam's rib, He made woman. From man God formed woman. Woman is of the same nature as man; husband and wife form one being, and woman is dependent on man.' Repeat, 'woman is dependant on man.' Perhaps we could call it a 'free translation'. It bore a Dutch *Imprimatur* for May 1983. (An *Imprimatur* is given by a bishop to signify that the book contains nothing contrary to the faith). There was no reference to Genesis 1.

Genesis 1:26-27 reads:

God said, 'Let us make man in our own image, in the likeness of ourselves, and let them be masters of the fish of the sea, the birds of heaven, the cattle, all wild beasts and all reptiles that crawl upon the earth'. God created man in the image of himself, in the image of God he created him, male and female he created them.

This is the translation from the *Jerusalem Bible* which is the translation most commonly used in the Church liturgy. Yet in the Fourth Eucharistic Prayer this passage is freely paraphrased and all mention of woman omitted: 'You formed man in your own likeness and set him over the whole world to serve you, his creator, and to rule over all creatures.' This is pure patriarchy alive and flourishing in the Church at the end of the twentieth century. It is unintentional, no doubt – which only serves to show how deeply rooted patriarchy is in the subconsciousness of modern churchmen.

However, some churchmen give us cause for hope:

The state of submission and oppression to which women are subjected in the world constitutes a sinful situation, something to correct. The Church must, in fidelity to the word of God, recognise the modern feminist movement as a positive reality. We are dealing, on the whole, with an advance in civilization; it is a forward step in the establishment of the Kingdom (Bishop Lebez, of Canada, 1980 Synod).

REFLECTIVE PAUSE

Patriarchy reasserted itself early in the life of the Church. List evidence of the influence of partriarchy in the Church today.

# SIX

# Patriarchy and Men

Patriarchy is a social system based on male privilege and power, in which women are regarded as secondary, created for the service of men. Patriarchy depends on hierarchy, on relationships of domination-subordination, on ranks, titles, 'correct' dress. Yet most men believe their masculine role in life is the natural outcome of their sex; they do not recognise it is the result of socialization.

At first glance it would appear that patriarchy has the dice well loaded in favour of men, but a little research will show that not all men are winners under patriarchy. It varies from culture to culture, and as feminist awareness has awakened within the Western culture, what follows is the outcome of the study of men in Western society.

Here we find that the demands patriarchy places on boys are, in some respects, far more inhibiting than those placed on girls. In Western society small 'tom-boys' are indulged, and as girls grow older they now have a wider choice of careers and dress. It is acceptable for a woman to act in the 'masculine' mode, but not for a man to behave in 'feminine' ways. In some families, little boys are still discouraged from playing with dolls and are forced into rough and tumble games, taught to 'fight their corner' and unrealistically expected to prepare for the role of sole breadwinner.

While visiting a retirement home in Dublin this year, I saw a young father bring in his four-year-old son to visit a relative. They had just been in a minor crash and the child was still upset and close to tears, but the father ordered him 'to pull himself together'. An old lady called the boy over, asked him if he had been frightened, and had he felt like crying. She told him that she too had been scared when in a crash once. As he wiped away tears she gave him a reassuring hug. His father called him back, shook him, and told him 'to behave like a man'. If that child had been a girl how would the young father have acted?

The 'masculine' is, according to the stereotype, intelligent, strong, courageous, in control, non-emotional, witty and a leader. This is the idol boys subconsciously compare themselves to, and so are left feeling a failure. As adults, many men are left robotised at assembly-lines, behind desks, on the parade ground, so much so that men are often compared to autistic children who, unable to relate, become fixated on objects. Authority roles are still regarded mainly as the preserve of men, millions of whom are unable to cope and so become stressed, as many a secretary knows. In a less competitive, more humane world of cooperation these men would function adequately.

Western men express concern about the 'women's problem', 'the 'black problem'; they are not aware that the white,

Western, middle-class man is the problem, and the source of our current sexist and racist problems. Feminists believe that the self-deception of men is greater than that of women and that patriarchy is in the last phase of destroying our humanity and our environment. On the other hand, the more hopeful of our social analysts see in the present world chaos the death throes of patriarchy.

The following paragraphs may appear negative, so I would like to emphasise that all is not gloom. Today, many young parents are trying to bring their children up in non-sexist ways, valuing people of other races and aware of injustices in public life. Even so, it is important at this stage in time to look back and try to understand the effect a patriarchal upbringing has had on us.

## Childhood

Many feminists hold that children were brought up within different cultures according to their sex. Little girls were trained to be dependent and nurturing, while boys were trained to be self-reliant and competitive. Yet nursery teachers tell us that little boys are the more sensitive to beauty, the more caring, the more easily upset if they hurt you. While boys were being taught to stand up for themselves, little distinction was made between aggression and defence. We have a society of aggressively trained men, and still we fail to provide our girls with the skills of self-defence. No doubt, it is presumed that their men folk will protect them.

As small boys were socialised into 'acting like a man', they were forbidden to use the healing process of tears. Instead we heard, 'Stop crying, or I'll give you something to cry about.' Their only defense was to numb their feelings, for when you are numb you feel no urge to take action.

Whenever I meet men at seminars, I hear their childhood memories of swaggering, dry-eyed, around the school-yard after a punch-up from the bullies, or clenching their teeth to prevent a howl when getting 'ten of the best' across the hand. Ridicule, beatings and rejection were the methods used, by both adults and peers, to force conformity to 'masculine' standards, with the result that it was much harder for a boy to come through childhood undamaged. Three times as many boys as girls needed the help of a psychologist during their early formative years.

'Boys will be boys', as one feminist observed, means 'Boys must be boys'. So long as aggression is admired and seen as a male birthright, boys will be booby-trapped with the suppressed emotions of anger, fear, and a sense of inadequacy. Then, in manhood, the day comes for some when even a slight irritation can cause an explosion, and violence erupts. This approach to training boys is the cause of many of our social problems.

## Violence

Many aggressively trained men find their outlet in sports, in politics, or in the money markets. Patriarchy values competition, casting man against man. It has even taken over in the world of classical music which is structure for failure as only the few can win. Violent men are the normal by-product of a patriarchal culture. The gentle non-aggressive men are the misfits, but they only fail to fit into patriarchy.

We need to ask why our society labels as wimps or gay, men who are gentle. Feminist men say that the persecution of gay men has nothing to do with their sexual orientation, but with their refusal to conform. Gay men treat women with respect, are no threat to them, and, free of sexual harassment, can work or socialise with women as colleague or friend.

Recently, four men entered a Dublin pub. One had just been told his wife had three months to live. He wept. While two of the men went to get drinks, the third man put his arm around his friend's shoulder. Immediately, several men got off their bar stools and proceeded to punch them. What is wrong with men that they feel threatened when confronted by a gesture of tenderness between man and man?

The capacity for violence has been institutionalised and men are expected to kill on command. I was in a war where a cease-fire was declared. In a nearby town, the soldiers from both sides came out and played football. Then the order was reversed and the soldiers separated to collect their guns and start firing at each other again. We read of young soldiers from opposite sides dying on the battlefield in each other's arms. Soldiers are meant to be heros, not to break down under stress; but many do, and are shot by the firing squad.

Around our planet today the killings continue – in Northern Ireland, in Bosnia, in South Africa, in Somalia, in Iraq, in Lebanon, in Cambodia, in El Salvador to name but a few places. Eventually peace has to be negotiated. We need honest answers as to what part the violence plays in these negotiations. In South Africa and in South America mothers are uniting and proclaiming, 'I did not bear my son in order for him to kill your son.' Feminist mothers are calling out: 'Let our sons go free.'

Violence becomes more personalised in the act of rape. Rape, it is said again and again, is not a response to the sexual urge, but is fired by the urge to dominate, to control, to demean another. Today, there is a growing concern for the victims of rape, but it is important to stress that rape is not a woman's problem. She is the victim. Nor can it be held that women provoke rape by their behaviour and their dress. Bed-ridden women of ninety are raped, toddlers of eighteen months are raped, young men and boys are raped. No. Rape is the outcome of men's problems. Some men's feminist groups, aware of this fact, are studying ways to prevent men seeking an outlet in rape.

Inadequate patriarchal men often associate 'masculinity' with sexual activity, and will turn to pornography or prostitution for a sexual outlet in which there is no need to relate to a woman. They use women, like drugs, to anaesthetise themselves against their inner sense of frustration.

Generations of Catholic girls were brought up to believe

that they were responsible for the sexual sins of men. In marriage this placed a dreadful burden on the wife. The presumption was that men were sexually compulsive and unable to exercise sexual self-control. These ideas were still being disseminated at a parents' meeting in 1992. When some of the senior boys heard about it they were horrified, and felt dehumanised by such theories.

## Family

The family is one of the main arenas for masculine violence. Being the authority figure at home buffers a man against failure in the work-place. Today, in the cases of abuse brought before our courts, we are at last getting a glimpse of the depth of some men's frustration, which they feel free to release in the hitherto closed world of the nuclear family. These men are not sick; they are the normal flotsam of a culture structured to produce so many patriarchal failures.

For many men the roles of producer, provider and protector are more than they have the ability to sustain, and so we have 'divorce Irish style' when such men desert their families and go to England. Or there are men who have carried the roles successfully for twenty years, and then suddenly find themselves made redundant and are unable to cope with what for them is 'loss of face'. In Birmingham I met Irishmen who, in their forties, were made redundant and had gone to England in search of work, but found that they were there considered too old. It was heartbreaking to see them deteriorate as they moved from hostel to hostel, avoiding the Catholic ones, and feeling too ashamed to go home. Such was the effect of our patriarchal culture on them.

At the other end of the scale, there are men who resent the bread-winner role, believing they have been trapped into providing their wives with a 'free dinner ticket' for life. Then there is an older generation of husbands who keep their wives dependent as a boost to their own egos. I am not now considering the role of women in the home or in public life, but rather the effects of our patriarchal system on some men, so that is where my focus will remain.

Marriage, for many men, is often secondary to their work, so that wives fail to get the companionship they had expected. When they plead with their husbands not to overwork, to take better care of their health, the usual response is, 'I'm doing it for you and the family. You will be left comfortable when I'm gone.' Most millionaires in the United States, I'm told, are women – widows of workaholics who died young. It is claimed that most divorce cases are filed by women, which suggests that women are looking for more than financial security from men today.

Men who were discussing these matters at a seminar agreed that the glorification of the traditional role of bread-winner was destructive of family life. They said it caused fathers to lose contact with their children, to feel alien at home, and so drove them to seek fulfilment through their work or outside activities. To enable fathers share more in family life they suggested the provision of more part-time work, and job-sharing.

For many adults, parenting and homemaking roles have to be worked at. Some men insist that child-minding and house-work come naturally to women. This attitude can be very oppressive for the women who know that, for them, they do not. At women's groups I have heard many women share their experience of how, after they had successfully given birth, they then had a difficult time learning to be a mother. Men, like women, need the experience of caring for infants and so be brought in touch with their own gentleness. Parenting can be very humanising.

Joint parenting is urgently needed when we hear that 'mothering' is the root cause of many men's inability to form mutual relationships with women. The theory is that after years of intensive mothering boys have to break away from the loved parent to find their role model elsewhere. Apparently, this causes an early distrust of women. Girls never have to go through this traumatic break in the mothering relationship. It is said that the mother 'love-trap' men suffer from affects their relationship with women, as no wife or girl-friend can be expected to give the same unconditional love of a mother. If this is true, then joint parenting would seem to be essential. At present, some men make no meaningful decisions about their lives either at home or at work.

## Work

Patriarchy identifies a man with his position. What counts is the job you have, not the kind of person you are. Even though the roles of producer, provider and protector are respected, it is the role and not the man that is honoured. When men are unemployed, made redundant, or retired many lose their sense of importance to the community, and so become ill, and sometimes commit suicide.

On the job, men are expected to be task- not people-oriented and are encouraged to suppress their personal feelings. As a result they can lose touch with their own bodies, not recognise the first signs of illness, and, as we know, many die 'suddenly' of heart attack. The pressure can be so great that some men are driven to see their colleagues as potential rivals and this leaves them isolated from each other. Feminists are asking men to re-examine their priorities in life and to stop evaluating themselves by the size of their pay-packets.

## The Church

Christian feminism is not just about sexist oppression, but about liberating men and women from the sin-trapped structures and attitudes that come from patriarchy and not from the Gospels. Church tradition has not helped men to value their tender qualities.

A priest psychologist who worked with seminarians noticed that the young men who entered usually had a developed sense of compassion and self-giving, but that by the time they had completed their training these qualities had been super-seded by concern for 'correct form' and visible signs of achievement. Young men who entered religious communities soon discovered that the only acceptable emotion was anger. One could express outrage, but not great delight, affection, or vulnerability. Over the centuries episcopal leaders, commissioned by Jesus to nourish the community, introduced thrones into the places of worship and replaced the Christ-term 'feed' with 'rule'. They confirmed young girls and boys as 'soldiers of Christ' and told them they were members of the Church Militant. Traditionalists perceive these developments as being in accordance with the will of God. Christian feminists see them as conditioned by a patriarchal society.

Through their questioning, women have awakened men to their own problems. For these are not 'women's problems', but human problems and Church problems. The man conditioned by patriarchy has undergone a mutilation of spirit. Therefore, it is up to Christian men to turn their backs on entrenched patriarchal values and forge a more Christlike identity that would model a new image of manliness for their sons. It requires real strength to refuse to conform, and even more to resist evil when it is presented as respectability. It has been said that, if you remove money, power and sex, men no longer know how to motivate themselves. Many have yet to learn that their own inner spirituality will provide the generating power they need.

Men's liberation requires the liberation of women, just as

the liberation of women depends on the liberation of men. To relegate women to subservient roles is not good for women, nor is it good for men, and it is a distortion of the Christ vision. Most women want to love men, to live side by side with them, sharing the burdens, the responsibilities, as well as the achievements. They ask men to recognise their fear of the competent woman for what it is – an infantile response to the women in their childhood. As one woman expressed it: 'Look at me. I am not your mother; I am not your elder sister or your junior teacher. Nor am I your servant or your pet. I am your peer.'

Despite the distortions of patriarchy, many men have miraculously managed to survive with most of their humanity intact. One recent convert to feminism tells how for years she could not understand the need for a women's movement. She had grown up in rural Ireland where she learned to fear the women in her life: her domineering mother and aunts, and the teachers and nuns who taught her. She had found the latter cruel and authoritarian. On the other hand, her father and uncles were kindly men, non-judgemental and compassionate. It was not until she studied the Gospels and became a missionary engaged in pastoral work with the clergy that she began to understand the need for a feminist approach in the Church.

When a man has done all that our patriarchal society expects of him as a colleague, a husband, a father, or a priest, and still feels a great dissatisfaction within, then the time for his conversion to feminist attitudes has come.

**The healing process**

The first step for a man to take in the healing process is to recall his early childhood, his first feelings of awe, his first acts of gentleness, and to reconnect with that small boy. Next it is necessary to get in touch with his feelings, and to acknowledge his need for affection, to be understood. Three times Jesus asked Peter, 'Do you love me?' Today that is a difficult question for a man to ask of another, even if the other is his son.

The more we heal the less need we have to hurt others. So it is time to give up the ridicule, to acknowledge the great diversity among boys, and to encourage them to be 'their own man' irrespective of the demands of patriarchy. We need to redefine for them our concepts of success.

Many kindly, well-intentioned men who consider them-selves to be pro-feminist, believe that all that women need is time and space to catch up on men. They fail to realise that women have an alternate wealth of experiences and insights to contribute for the betterment of the Church and society. These men are still trapped in the patriarchal notion that man is the norm. It is such men who require the time and space. But as one frustrated woman asked, 'How long? Another two thousand years?'

There is an urgent need for Christian men to reject outright the notion that it is part of God's plan that men should dominate women. They need to be prepared to step side-ways, to invite women on to decision making boards, and to accept them as co-partners. If they meet resistance from other men, then it has been suggested that they step outside the portals of privilege and join the women. Joan Chittister, O.S.B., tells the story of an ecumenical group that met in a monastery. When the time came for the liturgy, the men were invited into the church, while the women were asked to go to the gallery. The men, including the priests among them, decided to join the women. Their action caused the authorities to open the church to the whole group. These men understood that Christian feminism means accepting the fact that sex, race or class can no longer separate us, for we are all one in Jesus, the Christ.

REFLECTIVE PAUSE

1. Suppose you had been born of the opposite sex. List ways in which your childhood would have differed. List the difference it would make to your life today.
2. List some of the ways in which women collude with patriarchy, and so keep men in authority roles, and under pressure.

# SEVEN

# The Mystery We Call God

We have all been taught that God is pure Spirit. Yet, because of the images and language commonly used by Christians to express the inexpressible, many believers take it for granted that God is male. Irish missionaries have, in the past, travelled Europe and the rest of the world smashing 'pagan idols', and replacing them with a mental idol in the form of 'an old man with a white beard'. Even today, if you mention to a group of adults that there is no 'old man in the sky', some will conclude that you are denying the existence of God. They have literalised the metaphor 'Father'.

**Our Father**

In calling God 'Father' Jesus was inviting us into a more intimate relationship with the Divine Spirit. In fact, he used, not the term 'father' but 'Abba' which is more intimate. In using that term, Jesus set aside the austere patriarchal concept of fatherhood. 'Abba' as used by Jesus is a liberating image; but it has been taken over, changed to 'Father' and so the original flavour of the term used by Jesus was lost. Such is the conclusion of many biblical scholars. Several studies have been made to show the growth in the use of the term 'Father'.

The first Gospel, that of Mark, which was written around 64 A.D., uses the term four times. Luke uses it fifteen times, and Matthew forty-nine times. By the time John was written, possibly as late as 100 A.D. , it was used one hundred and nine times.

As the 'Father' metaphor came to be more commonly used, it acquired the overtones of the *paterfamilias* of the Greco-Roman cultures. Here the father had full power over the life and death of his family and household. The authority of the father was seen as of divine right, and rebellion against the father was regarded as rebellion against God.

## Language

Gregory Nazianzus (329 A.D.) taught that the terms 'father and son' as used in describing the Trinity, are metaphors, and that they refer to relationship, not to nature. We use metaphors because we have no other way in which to express the mystery that is God. These metaphors try to tell us that God is not solitary. They denote community, friendship, diversity, love, mutuality as belonging to the inner life of the Godhead. Therefore, the more we learn to love and relate in mutuality, the more we will understand the God mystery.

Unfortunately for women, the metaphors are male, thus implying that maleness is of the essence of God. Even the word 'Spirit' does not escape. The Hebrew *ruach* (translated 'spirit') is feminine, but the corresponding Greek word (*pneuma*) is neuter. In Latin the term is masculine (*spiritus*).

So, English-speaking Christians are left with three masculine metaphors to image divine relationships.

This language question is by no means a trivial issue, because the way we image God influences not only our attitudes and behaviour towards self but also towards others. A 'Father God' justifies paternalism and dependence among adults. A warlike God justifies our aggression against other peoples. In war bishops from both sides have blessed the troops and believed their cause was just.

A compassionate God helps us to be more accepting of others. Today, the image of God as love is influencing a younger generation. It is interesting to note that in the West the image of God as Judge remained dominant for centuries, while the Eastern Church was more familiar with the image of God as Physician.

At a theological forum a Western woman theologian said that by attributing the male sex to God, our male theologians were in a subtle way inferring that God is more a man than a woman; that to be male was the better of the two ways of being human. It required an Oriental theologian to widen our smug Western level of awareness. She stood up and declared: 'It is not just the constant image of a male God that offends me. It is the fact that it is a white, male God, a white, male, high-class God.' Our image of a white patriarchal God not just enabled us to condone sexism, but also racism, classism, colonialism and clericalism.

## Jesus

I am often asked if Christian feminists have a problem with the fact that Jesus was a man. The answer is 'No'. The problem arises when Church authorities rate the maleness of Jesus to be of greater importance than his humanity. For example, the most recent argument against the ordination of women is the fact that Jesus was a man.

In the various translations of the Bible the incarnation is described as: 'The Word was made flesh', 'The Word became man','The Word became a human being' (John 1:14). In the story of Paul's conversion, we are told that he got documents from the High Priest entitling him to arrest any followers of Jesus, 'both men and women', and to bring them to Jerusalem. On his way to carry out this task, he heard a voice call out: 'Saul, Saul, why do you persecute me?' 'Who are you ,Lord?', he asked. 'I am Jesus, whom you persecute' (Acts 9:1-5). Obviously Jesus has no problem identifying himself with the women among his followers.

It would appear suspect that while the Church tradition has no problem imaging Jesus as a fish, a lamb, bread and wine, it shirks away from identification with a woman, an identification made by Jesus himself.

## 'Mother God'

The Jewish Bible is rich in mother images of God.

First, there are the birth metaphors. 'From whose womb did the ice water come, and who gave birth to the frost?' (Job

38:29). Later Paul will refer to the cosmic womb of God. Isaiah used the image several times, as in the text: 'I have been quiet and held myself back; but now I will cry out like a woman in labour, I will strain and pant' (42:14). In Deuteronomy 32:18, God complains at having been forgotten, after bringing the people forth in 'labour pains'. The Revised Standard Version has: 'You forgot the God who gave you birth.' In 1968 the Jerusalem Bible translated the passage as 'unmindful now of the God who fathered you.' This is the version most commonly used in the liturgy.

Next there are the comforting, protecting images. 'As a child who is comforted by his mother, so will I comfort you' (Isaiah 66:13). 'I will fall upon them like a bear robbed of her cubs' (Hosea 13:8). In some passages God is presented as a midwife. 'Shall I help bring to birth, and yet not let you bring forth?' (Isaiah 11:9). 'You are the one who took me from my mother's womb, and laid me safely on my mother's breast' (Psalm 22:9). In Psalm 131:2, the writer again compares God to a mother. 'I have found ease and peace for my spirit, just as a child does at the mother's breast.'

As can be seen from these passages, most of the biblical images centre on a woman's experience of motherhood, for patriarchy equates woman with child-bearing and rearing. Today, there is a tendency to romanticise motherhood, so that often a woman's real experience of mothering is not addressed. There are women who have been made mothers against their will; and there are women who abandon their children. There are inadequate mothers who cannot protect their children from abuse; and there are possessive mothers who make their children psychologically dependent on them. Psychologists report that there are many women and men who can trace their adult problems back to a mother for whom they now feel nothing but resentment. Then there are the wise, competent mothers who not only provide food and emotional stability, but give their children intellectual nourishment as well.

However, women cannot be defined by motherhood alone. Many women never become mothers. So another look at the Bible will show God represented by wisdom which is also a female image. The Greek word for wisdom is *sophia*, and the image of the Sophia-God was in widespread use in the early Eastern Church. Unfortunately, this feminine aspect of God was eventually applied to Mary, and so God was again left with only the male images commonly in use.

The value of using female images of God today is to free the mind from any residue of literalism left over from our childhood perceptions of God as 'an old man'. Also, in order to acknowledge that a woman's body is a worthy image for the Divine. As language and metaphors are of such importance, some feminists believe it is a cop-out to concentrate on female images at this stage of awareness raising, when a more all-encompassing task awaits our theologians.

**New images**

It is the task of theology to help us understand our human experience of God. Theological language codifies our spiritual insights. But so far, the spiritual insights of women have gone unacknowledged in this process. Some Christian feminists believe that there is a need to reinterpret our understanding of the Divinity as our present definitions are flawed by patriarchy. Patriarchy still presents the old order of sin, and prevents the living out of the full meaning of reconciliation in Christ, as expressed through a community of equals.

Genesis 1:27 can be our starting place. 'God created human beings; in his own image he made them; male and female he created them.' Here we are back to the Trinitarian insight that at the core of the Divinity we find community and mutual relationships. Women theologians point out that every human being has a complete respiratory, digestive, blood and nervous system, but only half a genital system. To generate life, female and male are needed. To image God, female and male are needed. It is not redemptive to diminish the image of God in women, to regard them as 'objects of sin', and to legitimise their subordination to men.

Sexism is wrong, not because it suggests some women are stupid, seductive or irresponsible. There are such women. Sexism is wrong because it regards women as secondary to men. Women were created equal, were equally redeemed, equally baptized into Christ, and are equally destined for heaven. Therefore, as women are made in the image of God, then God can be imaged by a woman, and so the 'Mother God' image is justified.

But as we have seen, to tamper with embedded images of God can threaten reality for some people. Yet, if our images are oppressive rather than empowering, then faith demands that we relinquish our false images in order to come to know God more truly. When Jesus referred to God as 'Abba' he opened up for us a whole new relationship of intimacy with the Divine. Somehow, we need through our images to regain that 'at homeness' with God.

Sallie McFague, in her book *Models of God*, suggests along with 'Mother', the metaphors 'Love' and 'Friend'. Friendship is the most free of all the relationships between adults. It implies mutuality, affection, trust, shared interests, and it breaks down the patriarchal barriers of sex, race, class and age. New images of God would need to avoid sexism, or any overtones of a domination-subordination relationship.

Feminist theology, while liberating for many, can be disturbing for some, for it questions the very language and concepts we use in order to image God to ourselves. What is at stake here is the truth about God. Sometimes our images have served to turn people away from God. As one would-be convert asked a missionary at the end of a sermon: 'Would you worship a God like that?' One of the oldest Council Fathers at Vatican II one day remarked, 'The God the atheists don't believe in, I don't believe in either.' Urged on by the sight of 'a harvest' waiting, Christian feminist scholars continue to search the Scriptures, to study creation and human experience in an effort to make more intelligible the Mystery we call 'God'.

## REFLECTIVE PAUSE

1. What words come to mind when you hear the term God? What words come to mind when you hear the term Goddess? Do your two lists differ? Why?

2. Our image of God comes from our experience of a patriarchal society. We image God in our own likeness. But suppose we lived in an isolated island society based on mutuality and cooperation; how then would we image the Divinity?

3. Sit back and image God as a woman. Talk to her prayerfully for three minutes. How do you feel after the experience?

   Remember that in our public liturgies women are obliged to relate to God in the image of a man.

# EIGHT

# Inclusive Language

A living language grows and develops as words change their meaning and new words appear. Language is never neutral. It reflects the values of a society at any given time, and not only helps to express a culture, but it influences and shapes that culture as well. Because language is such a powerful tool it needs to be used with the greatest precision.

With the growth in feminist awareness, a number of women came to realise that in some languages they were almost invisible. English is one such language, using as it does the term 'man' to stand for the whole human race. The Irish language is not so exclusive; it has no equivalent for 'mankind'; the Irish term is *an cine daonna*, that is, 'all the people'.

For the last twenty years there has been a growing lobby asking for greater sensitivity in the use of language, so much so that in the English-speaking world governments, business and media corporations have set guidelines for the use of inclusive language in their statements. This has caused distress to many, both women and men, who believe the integrity of the English language is under attack. However, as one woman exclaimed, 'It is nonsense to say that "man" includes women when it so blatantly does not.' An example from a modern philosopher will prove her point. He wrote: 'Man's basic needs are life, food, access to the female … '

In the Bible the translators go further and use the term 'people' for men only. 'Then he [Moses] said to the people, "Be ready for the third day; do not go near any woman".' (Exodus 19:14, Jerusalem Bible version) But the situation becomes more questionable when the title 'Christian' is used exclusively. An Intercessary Prayer from the Divine Office for Wednesday Evening in Lent reads: 'Grant that Christians will prove brothers to the sick.'

Perhaps, the most extraordinary example comes from the Liturgy of the Eucharist. The Jerusalem Bible, which is the text used in the Liturgy, translates from the three Gospel accounts of the Last Supper as follows:

'For this is my blood of the covenant, which is to be poured out for many for the forgiveness of sins' (Matthew 26:28).

'This is my blood, the blood of the covenant, which is to be poured out for many' (Mark 14:24)

'This cup is the new covenant in my blood which will be poured out for you' (Luke 22:20).

Note now the change from inclusive to exclusive language made by the liturgist who composed the central prayer of the Mass: 'This is the cup of my blood, the blood of the new and everlasting Covenant. It will be shed for you and for all men so that sins may be forgiven.' This wording was used in all four of the Eucharistic Prayers when the new English Missal was first published. The situation has been amended since with official recognition (in a Vatican Letter, 12 January 1985) that the Eucharistic Prayer should read 'for you and for all' instead of 'for all men'.

The International Commission for English in the Liturgy has asked liturgists to avoid sexist, racist, and anti-semetic language. This is a useful reminder to all the clergy to become more sensitive in the use of language both in readings and sermons. Their statement declares:

> The failure of much liturgical and theological language adequately to recognise the presence of women seems effectively to exclude them from full and integral participation in the life of the Church, and this exclusion can prevent the whole Church from experiencing the fullness of Christian Community.

Some suggested changes made in the report are to substitute 'forebearers' for 'forefathers', 'humankind' for 'mankind', 'community' for 'brotherhood', 'friends' for 'brethren'. Besides, the document also advises the addition of women – examples would be 'brothers and sisters', 'men and women'.

The Church authorities are faced with a dilemma: if they change the liturgical language they will give offence to some, and if they fail to change it they will alienate others. There is no doubt that inclusive language expresses the 'new creation' in which all are one in Christ, and therefore should be the language of a Christian community. 'As the Church prays, so it believes' (*lex orandi, lex credendi*) is a long-standing insight.

At present the language of the Church reflects the insights and awareness of only half its membership. This means that the inclusive language question is not just about linguistics, but has grave theological and social implications as well. It has been suggested that if bishops and priests were, for just one day, to pray 'for us women and our salvation ... ', they might come a little nearer to understanding the sense of alienation experienced by many women at our liturgical celebrations. The fact that the Vatican has insisted that the English translation of the new *Catechism of the Universal Church* be in exclusive language is a cause of utter bewilderment to many Catholic women and men, including clergy.

The use of inclusive language is a very straightforward way of starting to reverse discrimination against women, both in the Church and in society at large. It is important to remember that a feminist attitude includes the sensitive use of language regarding people with disabilities, and those of different nationality, race or creed. Once a person begins to become aware, they find their awareness continues to expand into areas hitherto unthought of; but at this point they must practise tolerance, as no one can ever become so aware that they will not give offence at times. One can only trust that a basic good-will towards all will be felt and accepted. Realizing this, I smiled, at a prayer meeting, recently. The focus was on raising awareness of the environmental responsibilities entrusted to us by God, but unthinkingly the composer of the prayers had used sexist language.

Feminism is developing its own vocabulary in an effort to articulate meanings not prevalent in our male-dominated language. For example, interdependence is of core importance to feminists, so words like 'bonding', 'enabling', 'empowering', 'becoming', 'mutuality' are in common use among them. It is interesting to note that physicists tell us that relational-energy is the source of all living things.

The language we use reveals our attitudes. Politicians have often included women in the phrase 'minority groups'; yet, when you come to think about it, you remember women form over half the population of the world. Again, take the phrase 'the man in the street', it really has no female equivalent, the nearest we get is 'the woman on the street', and that has no male equivalent. To bring home the fact of the invisibility of women in the English language an experiment was carried out on adults and children. A passage was read in exclusive language. Then the listeners were asked to draw the scene. Only male figures appeared in their pictures.

The mention of children reminds me of the feminist mother who overheard her six-year-old daughter tell her playmates that boys were better than girls. Horrified, the mother called the child and asked who had put such an idea into her head. 'You did, Mummy. Last Wednesday when you were teaching me how to play Rummy, you said that the Kings were better than the Queens.' I have a dream. It is this: for ten years a moratorium is declared on Kings, the Queen is the top card. I can see patriarchy crumbling as card-players from Las Vegas to Monte Carlo stretch out their hands to collect the winnings, only to be reminded of a new reality!

My favourite language-story concerns a public figure in London. He was introducing the chairperson for the evening and called her the chairman, explaining that his tongue had trouble getting around such a clumsy word as chairwoman. When the talk was over and it was time for questions, a young girl got up and addressed her question to the public figure. 'You said your tongue had trouble getting around the word "chairwoman".' 'Yes, yes,' he pooh-poohed. 'I wondered,' she persisted, 'if your tongue has difficulty getting around the word "charwoman"?' I am told he had the grace to blush.

Feminists seek honesty and consistency. If the phrase 'God loves all men' is inclusive, then they ask, 'How inclusive is the phrase, "Let the best man get the job"?' Only a few years ago, here in Dublin, a man tried to challenge in the courts the legality of Mary Robinson standing for election as President of Ireland. He based his case on the fact that the Constitution was written in exclusive language and so had not allowed for a woman President. (He must have forgotten that the Constitution was also written in Irish, and that the Irish text has precedence if there is a dispute about meaning.)

Language is a powerful tool, it requires constant evaluation as words come or go, or change their meaning. A language reflects a society's attitudes. In the same way the language used by the Church reveals or conceals the fullness of Christ's message.

## REFLECTIVE PAUSE

Would you consider inclusive language of importance today? Why?

# NINE

# Mary of Nazareth

It comes as a surprise to many Catholics when they discover how few are the references to Mary in our Scriptures. There are, of course, the familiar Infancy Narratives that tell the Christmas story. But they were written in a particular Hebrew literary form and require special interpretation. They were written over sixty years after the birth of Jesus; some scholars claim they were added to the Gospels even later. Matthew made Joseph the focus of these stories and centred his narrative on five prophecies. Luke, on the other hand, focused on Mary and presented her as the 'Daughter of Sion', a Jewish metaphor standing for the People of Israel. As the Infancy Stories deserve a complete Marian study in themselves, I will not, for the purposes of this book, pursue them any further.

In the record of the public life of Jesus, Mary is mentioned no more than twice by any of the four evangelists.

In Matthew's Gospel, there is a passage (12:46-50) which describes Mary and her family seeking Jesus and another passage (13:53-58) describes Jesus being rejected by the people of Nazareth, with the comment, 'It is the carpenter, Mary's son.'

In the Gospel according to Mark the same two incidents are

recorded at 3:20-35 and at 6:1-6.

When we look at Luke's account, we find the same incidents listed. At 8:19-21 we have the account of the mother of Jesus and his brothers coming looking for him. The story of his rejection at Nazareth is also told (4:16-30), with one change: Mary is not mentioned; instead the people ask: 'Is not he the son of Joseph?' (4:23). In his account of the early Church, Luke mentions Mary once more. She is at prayer among the disciples in the Upper Room (Acts 1:14).

John's Gospel contains a lot of symbolism, and again Mary is mentioned twice. Mary plays a significant role in all that the Marriage at Cana stood for (John 2:1-12). And as Jesus approaches death Mary and the 'beloved disciple' were given into each other's care at the foot of the cross (John 19:25-27). This is seen as a symbol of the new community of faith that takes precedence over family ties. John is the only evangelist who presents Mary at the cross. In the other Gospels Mary is not mentioned among the group of women present.

Although Paul never refers to Mary by name, we find that in Galatians he states: 'he was born of a woman' (4:4).

That completes the references to Mary contained in the Christian canon of Scripture. Interestingly, the Koran, the sacred book of Islam, has seven very reverent references to Maryam, the mother of Jesus.

Actually, there is one other reference to Mary, though she is unnamed. Jesus was preaching when a woman in the crowd got carried away with emotion and called out, 'Blessed is the womb that carried you, and the breasts that gave you suck' (Luke 11:27). Jesus did not brush this woman's enthusiasm aside; instead he took time to instruct her. He assigned no importance to the biological relationship but explained that blessings belonged to those who, on hearing the word of God, acted upon it. His mother was to be honoured for her faith not her biological functions. For it was Mary's faith response to the Word of God that enabled her physical motherhood to take place, and which enfleshed God among us.

Jesus took advantage of another incident to elaborate on this teaching. This happening is reported in Mark's Gospel, 3:30-35. Jesus had returned to his home place with his disciples, and was kept so busy teaching that he had no time to eat. Meanwhile, teachers from Jerusalem had followed him north and were telling the people that he was possessed. Neighbours informed the family, and when they heard that 'he has gone mad,' they set out to take him away. When they reached the house in which he was teaching they asked for Jesus to be brought out. 'Your mother, and your brothers and sisters are here, and want to see you.' Jesus answered; 'Who is my mother and who are my brothers?' Then looking at those listening to him he said; 'Here are my mother and brothers. For whoever does God's Word is my brother, my sister and my mother.' Once again the teaching is clear. Blood relationships are not enough, they have to be transformed, include others, and become communities of faith.

Whenever I am asked by a group of women to introduce

them to Bible reflection, I often begin with this incident. We have read it through twice and go on to take perhaps ten minutes in silence to allow the scene become real for each one. I then ask them to share their thoughts with each other in twos. The buzz is energising. When it is time for the open sharing, there are generally one or two women who have decided that they have a son like Jesus. It goes something like this. He is in with a gang, is not eating properly, people are talking about him, and at thirty years of age he is still a worry to his mother. Praying through this very human, and not too dignified a situation, most of the women find that they have entered into a whole new relationship with Mary.

This sense of a shared faith with Mary arrived in Ireland with the Gospels. In early Celtic, Christian documents Mary is never presented as remote, celestial, raised up for us to pray to; rather, she is 'one of us', at prayer beside us, a 'companion on the way'. One bardic poet wrote that we are related to Jesus on his mother's side. 'He should have respect for his own, his mother and I have the same blood.' There is an intimacy in speaking to Mary, she is called *Mairenat* or Little Mother. Blathmac in the eighth century wrote inviting Mary to 'Come by me, Mary my love, and we will keen together.' Throughout the long poem with Mary by his side, he recalls her life with Jesus. Verse after verse, the Gospel story is told, then he sorrows with her as he remembers her Son's suffering and death. Keening with Mary is a feature of Celtic writing.

**Virgin mother**

Back on the Continent a different development was taking place, one with a considerable history. Ignatius, Bishop of Antioch, who was martyred in 117 A.D. wrote of Jesus as 'God born of Mary'. Justin, the martyr (165 A.D.) in writing on the prophecy 'A virgin shall conceive and give birth to a son, and he will be called Emmanuel, God with us' (Isaiah 7:14), taught that Mary conceived without intercourse. And still in the second century, a document which had wide circulation but never became part of Scripture, claimed that Mary gave birth miraculously without breaking her hymen. 'And it came to pass, that while she was by herself, Mary found to her amazement a small infant beside her. On looking at her body she found it was as it had been before she had conceived' (*Ascension of Isaiah*, 8)

So now the teaching was that Mary had conceived without a father, given birth without losing her physical virginity, and had no sexual intercourse throughout her marriage: she was the ever-virgin Mother of God. In the fourth and fifth centuries Ambrose, Augustine and Leo the Great declared that Mary's life-long virginity was part of her integrity. Jerome saw it as part of her redeemed humanity. The theory of the unbroken hymen causes offence to many mothers, who feel it demeans the sacredness of their own deliveries. It is thought that the Church Fathers believed the labour pains of child birth were the result of sin, and so would not associate them with Mary.

As the title 'God-bearer' (*Theotokos* in Greek), came more into use for Mary, Nestorius, Bishop of Constantinople, objected saying that Jesus had two personalities, a human and a divine, and that Mary gave birth only to the human. At the Council of Ephesus in 431 A.D., Nestorius was denounced, and the title 'Mother of God' was affirmed and applied to Mary. So by the middle of the fifth century Mary was exalted by the Church simply because of her biological relationship with Jesus. The fact that Jesus had played down this relationship and had given priority to oneness with him in a community of faith was ignored.

Throughout the fifth century the virginity of Mary continued to be questioned, to the fury of the hot-tempered scholar, Jerome. From 382 to 385 A.D., Jerome was secretary to Pope Damasus, and while in Rome he refuted the critics of Mary's virginity. From then on the perpetual virginity of Mary became a doctrine of the Church.

We might ask: Why at this time was the Church so concerned with the virginity of Mary? The reason may have been the fact that the true nature of Jesus was a matter for debate. Ephesus had declared that Jesus was fully human. Then in 451 A.D. the Council of Chalcedon confirmed the divinity of Christ. The biology prevailing at the time and handed down from Aristotle, led the Church Fathers to conclude that woman was a passive, physical container for the 'seed of life' which resided in man. By denying a human father to Jesus, it could be said that Mary received the 'seed of life' directly from God. This is yet another way of presenting God as male.

Some Christian feminists hold that the doctrine of the virginity of Mary is not concerned with the physical state of Mary, but with the nature of her Son. In the sixth century Leontius taught that the nature of Jesus did not depend on the virginity of Mary.

The Gospels speak of the 'brothers and sisters' of Jesus. Catholic tradition teaches that the terms refer to cousins. Some commentators even speculated that Joseph was a widower and that his previous marriage had provided Jesus with step-sisters and step-brothers. However, the Gospels use the Greek word *adelphos*, the same word which is used when referring to the relationship between Peter and Andrew, and also between James and John. However, Paul had already used the term in his letters when speaking of a spiritual brotherhood. In the case of Jesus, scholars are still at variance as to the correct interpretation.

Sts Ambrose and Bernard wrote with great respect and profundity when dealing with the role of Mary. But by the fourteenth century devotion to her had become sentimental. This may have been due to the influence of the 'courtly love' tradition found among knights, troubadours and poets. Mary became 'Our Lady' to whose honour some knights pledged their services. Luther, Zwingli and Calvin, who while honouring Mary did not exalt her, sought to curb some of the devotional excesses, but in response the Roman Church defended the popular elevation of Mary. Then came Jansen with his austere and rigorous teachings about sin and salvation. To counteract the fear of eternal damnation that such harsh attitudes instilled in the faithful, Sts Alphonsus de Ligouri and Louis de Montfort introduced a renewed devotion to Mary, based on her merciful intercession for all sinners. De Montfort entitled her the Mediatrix of all Graces.

Marian devotion peaked in the nineteenth and early twentieth centuries. All over Europe, Catholics reported visions of Mary. Between 1830 and 1932 her presence was witnessed in Paris, Rome, La Salette, Lourdes, Croatia, Bohemia, Normandy, Knock, Fatima, and Belgium. In Knock, Mary remained silent, but elsewhere the messages heard were conservative and expressed a fear of change. From 1831 on, the Miraculous Medal of Mary was worn. In 1854, the dogma of the Immaculate Conception was promulgated. In 1917, Maximilian Kolbe founded the Militia of the Immaculate Conception, and in 1921 Frank Duff started the Legion of Mary. In 1942 Pius XII consecrated the world to the Immaculate Heart of Mary. In 1950 the dogma of the Assumption of Mary was promulgated.

The 1960s brought the Council of Vatican II. There was a strong lobby of devotees who hoped to have Mary's role in the Church discussed in a separate document. They also asked for her to be declared Mediatrix of all Graces. The Council Fathers resisted the pressure and instead recommended a return to the Scriptures and to Mary as woman of faith. They declared that Jesus was our only Mediator and stressed Mary's dependence on Christ. Mary's role was discussed within the Constitution on the Church thus presenting her to us as a co-believer. The Celtic Church had got it right.

Later, Paul VI wrote *Marialis Cultus* in which he honoured Mary but warned against excessive devotions. Mary was to be our model of faith in action, and devotion to her was to include her Son, and to be based on the Scriptures and the liturgies. He also asked that the ecumenical dimension be remembered. The Pope attributed to 'popular writing' the difficulties many women experienced in regard to Mary, and he advised Catholics to respect the insights of the Protestant communities.

Teilhard de Chardin believed the cult of Mary served a real need as a counter-balance to a 'dreadfully masculinized' understanding of God. Christians deprived of female images of God turned to Mary, and applied to her the more tender aspects of the Deity. Mary was called Mother of Mercy and Mother of Consolation, while God retained the title 'Judge'. Yet Jesus told stories to emphasise that God is merciful, and he sent the Spirit to be our Consoler. However, popular devotion is not concerned with theological nuances. The devotees seek reassurance through signs and wonders. They are uncritical, and worship through prayers of petition and thanksgiving rather than of praise and often seem to disregard the sober face of official teachings.

Officially, women now have a more realistic model in Mary, and this leaves an older generation feeling betrayed in their devotion to her. Sometimes, older priests are at a loss to know what to preach. As recently as 1991, in a Dublin church, the congregation was told that Mary is the model for women, and Jesus the model for men. Notice the men are given the divine model. The truth is that Jesus models God incarnate for us all, and Mary is the model of a faithful believer for both men and women.

Traditional Marian devotion is the product of patriarchy, in which Mary was valued for her motherhood and virginity. A virgin-mother is an impossible model to emulate; it places perfection beyond the reach of women, and causes some to feel guilt-ridden. It is especially repugnant for many women to hear a man preach about Mary as the ideal woman who was meek, modest, submissive, and silent. The more Mary is idealised, the less respect is shown for the reality of ordinary women. The four dogmas concerning Mary proclaim her divine motherhood, her perpetual virginity, her immaculate conception, and her assumption. But in fact, only her mother-hood has an explicit basis in Scripture.

## A new Mariology

The evangelists never exalted Mary. They had no problem presenting her as bewildered, anxious, and struggling to understand her Son. Like him, she grew in wisdom and grace. Nor were they afraid to show her as having little influence among her townspeople. ' "Is not this Mary's son?" they asked, "Are not James, Joseph, Judas and Simon his brothers?" So they rejected him' (Mark 6:3).

Mary has to be seen within the Church, as a member of our worshipping community, not up on a pedestal facing us. There is no room for sentimentality or sensationalism which fails to lead us to a true understanding of her and our Christian commitment. For women, Mary is part of their sisterhood, and the liberation of women includes the liberation of Mary from false imaging. There is no doubt that in times past theology flirted with the idea of Mary as semi-divine. It is up to women to return to Mary her full humanity, her sexuality and her womanliness.

A new Mariology will see Mary as 'one of us', growing in faith, moving from unbelief to belief. A Marian leaflet, published by the Irish Bishops in 1987, supports this approach. 'Despite the doubt she [Mary] must have entertained and the fears she must have felt, she was the Lord's first and best disciple.' And, 'At no stage was she the timid, marginalised creature of occasional misrepresentation.'

For modern women, Mary's initiative and faith-in-action need to be stressed. Luke presented her as a young woman faced with a difficult choice. She did not hesitate to question the angel or to make the decision on her own. Later, we are told she was given to deep reflection, but at no time does she seem to be in awe of her Son. We see her encouraging him to act, going to his aid, and standing by his cross. Our final glimpse of her is at prayer among his disciples.

Christian feminists see in the dogma of the Immaculate

Conception an affirmation of sexuality as blessed. And in the dogma of the Assumption they see affirmed the goodness of the human body. For them, Mary, as a symbol, is a reminder that God can dwell in us. They image Mary as 'companion', and as 'wise woman' pondering on the mystery of God.

Meanwhile, there is a need to popularise the female images of God, found in the Bible, for by so doing we release Mary to become more fully herself, and enhance the dignity of all women. When the Church authorities acknowledge that women can image God and administer grace, then Mary will be allowed to take up her place among us. In thus freeing Mary we return to God the 'feminine' attributes which rightly belong to the Godhead. Then as in Genesis 1:27 we can present a truer image of the Divinity.

REFLECTIVE PAUSE

1. Invite Mary to your side, and ask her to tell you about her faith struggle. What did you learn?        (3 minutes)
2. Ask Mary to pray WITH you, that your faith may become more enlightened. How do you feel?        (3 minutes)

# A Grace for the Church

This book is written as an introduction to Christian feminism which, as I understand it, is simply the Gospel vision given to us by Jesus.

Christian feminism sees the concerns of women in the wider context of the concerns of the Church. Once we grasp the fact that the Gospel message has been brought to us through the interpretations of men, from their experiences of God and life in a patriarchal society, then we realise that the fullness of human reflection has not yet been acknowledged by the Christian community. The trivialising of women's experiences and insights is the cause of deep pain among women. It leaves them with a sense of alienation. A sexist priest cancels out the Good News for many women, who gradually leave a Church that they come to perceive as irrelevant to their lives. Christian feminists try to enable such women to focus on the Gospels and the wider Christian community and not to take too narrow a view of Church.

Sexism is part of original sin. It is not inate in us; we are born into a patriarchal culture and all of us, women and men, have unconsciously absorbed patriarchal attitudes. Patriarchy is not a clerical conspiracy against women, though some women seem to suspect it is. Therefore, there is an urgent need for the Christian community to acknowledge the distortions in Church attitudes brought about by patriarchy and to set about correcting them. But to do this the insights of feminism are needed. Christian feminism is a grace for the Church, a prophetic voice calling it to a more Christlike witness.

There is a popular saying: 'Feminists are not asking for a larger slice of the cake, they are asking for a whole new recipe.' One night, in Cork, I quoted this saying and at the end of the talk a woman in the audience stood up and said: 'Christian feminists are not asking for a larger slice of the cake, they are asking for the original recipe.'

This brings us back to Jesus and the Gospels. Christian feminists realise that it is only those who become aware who can bring about change, and that such awareness brings responsibility. They realise also that all change is scary, that it upsets the *status quo*. So naturally those who benefit from patriarchy have cause to feel anxious. For it is not a matter of an adjustment here and there; rather it is a thorough pruning job that is waiting to be done.

Traditionalists are comfortable with women who are servile, passive and devotional. It is the confident women with trained intellects and a sense of Christian mission that they perceive as a 'problem'. They need to sincerely ask themselves, Why? It is to be hoped that they will come to recognise Christian feminism as a source for renewal in the Church, as its scholars critique the past for us, recover the history of

Christian women, and reflect anew on Church teachings. It is up to Christian feminists not to impose, and thereby become as oppressive as patriarchy, but to follow the example of Jesus who proclaimed the message and lived its truths.

Peter himself had to learn that some of the teachings of his faith needed to be reconsidered. 'What God has purified may not be considered unclean' (Acts 11:5-9). That truth applied to animals. Today that same truth needs to be applied to women. 'Those whom God has baptized may not be considered unworthy.' Christian feminists do not suggest that by allowing women to take up leadership roles, the Church will become more holy. What they do maintain is that by so doing the Church will be enabled to witness to justice. The truths of feminism are the concerns not of women alone, but of the whole Christian community.

## The ever-unfolding plan of God

Again and again, Jesus said that we will be blessed, fulfilled if we 'hear the word of God and do it'. He assured us that God had 'counted the hairs of our heads', and knew when the smallest sparrow fell to the ground, that it was all part of the overall divine plan at work among us.

Frequently over the past few years I have come across references to the work of modern physicists, and heard statements such as: 'It is the physicists we have to turn to today for a greater understanding of God.' Then recently I saw a programme entitled *The Global Brain*. It is based on the book *The Awakening Earth* by Peter Russell. The programme began with a view of our earth revolving in space. Peter Russell, as narrator, said that the first astronauts from the U.S. and U.S.S.R., on seeing our globe suspended in space, returned to earth not as Soviets or Americans, but as Global people. They had become aware that we and all that exists on earth form one living organism.

Then followed an overview of the stages in evolution not as being an obvious ongoing process, but as having long periods of unobtrusive waiting for conditions to right themselves for the next evolutionary leap. Russell took us back to the Big Bang which threw out energy and light which eventually condensed into particles that came together to form atoms, and when the atoms attained sufficient complexity they formed molecules which in turn produced DNA, the long threads that are the stuff of life. All this took billions of years to evolve, as each new creation had to reach a certain stage of complexity before the next evolutionary leap could take place. 'The wheels of God grind slowly.'

With DNA on earth the bacteria cells appeared, then algae, and as these cells gathered together sponges were formed. The next great leap produced the fish and now for the first time the nervous system was protected by bone in the spine and skull. From now on, evolution concentrated on the nervous system – lizards, small mammals, dinosaurs, birds, right up to dolphins and whales came into being.

Meanwhile, other interesting things where happening on

earth. The temperature on earth steadied after millions of years and has stayed constant. Our planet should have burned out but all the living creatures on earth sent out sufficient gases to modify the sun's heat. Similarly, the salt washed into the sea should, over the millennia, have destroyed the oceans, but again the organisms in the depths were able to absorb sufficient salt to keep the level steady. These facts are important as they remind us that when earth seems threatened by some superabundance, e.g. the population, the Divine at work in nature seems to step in and provides for a modifying of the threat.

When humans finally evolved, our nervous system was so complex that we were able to reflect. The whole of the universe is inter-related and we are that part of the universe that has emerged with a spiritual capacity. From their study of the universe and its history of evolutionary patterns, some physicists have concluded that the next evolutionary leap will be in the area of human consciousness. As they look at what is happening around the world they perceive conditions readying themselves for the next creative leap. Already we have, through our satellites and computers, an information net-working system in place, so that ideas can now be communicated directly around the globe. In the past ideas were subject to distortions as they were communicated through word of mouth, or depended on the accuracy of scribes.

Today, human beings are linking mentally, meeting at a deeper spiritual level, working towards an united global consciousness. Just as previously cells clustered together and thus empowered made the next leap, so we humans are clustering together as never before, eg. in the United Nations, the European Union, the World Council of Churches.

It took the complexity of ten billion atoms to produce a cell, and of ten billion cells to produce a human brain, and so ten billion human consciousnesses meeting together to share positive ideas could generate sufficient life-giving energy to produce the next state of evolution on earth, that is, a global consciousness that will enable us live in harmony with each other and with our planet.

We are one living organism: when one part is abused, all suffer. In the human foetus brain cells develop and multiply from weeks ten to thirteen. There is such an explosion of brain cells that if it continued it would destroy the new human life, but miraculously at week thirteen the explosion stops and brain cells begin to link with each other and to send out interdependent messages. Peter Russell suggests that what is called our present 'population explosion' should reach its maximum around the early part of the new century and then level off leaving us with sufficient inter-communicating brain power to enable our next evolutionary leap into a more spiritually oriented life-style. But, of course, just as rogue cells form cancers, so brain power that entertains evil can destroy any hope of a continuing harmony among people. However, some social analysts see in the present world turmoil and wars, the death throes of patriarchy. At the end of the twentieth century we are all aware that the world is in crisis. The word 'crisis' suggests 'at a turning point'; it offers new opportunities for growth. Social commentatore have already labelled the 1980s as the 'Me Generation'. We are now in the 1990s preparing for a new milennium and we need to start now to make the shift from 'myself', 'my family', 'my nation' to a wider God-given consciousness of 'my global community'.

The human brain contains cells whose functions are still unknown to medics. Physicists observe that evolution is now directed towards developing human brain power and the spiritual capacity of humankind. If their observations are right, then I see the growth of feminist study-support groups and the net-working that takes place between them, as part of the plan of God unfolding among us. For each group is contributing to the build-up of human harmony and the shedding of sinful prejudices so that Christ's vision of a community healed of divisions based on sex, race and class can come into being. Peter Russell ended his programme with the thought that our next evolutionary leap will be an enter-prise into the Mystery we call 'God'.

### REFLECTIVE PAUSE

1. Does Christian feminism irritate, disturb, excite or em-power you ? Why?
2. What would be your next step in either refuting or promot-ing Christian feminism ?

# Starting a Study / Support Group

Some people experience a sense of isolation or aloneness when they first become aware of the truth of feminist thinking. It is then that a study-support group proves a great help. The group provides a safe place in which to explore new ideas. Here, each one is listened to as thoughts are shared and clarified, and this sharing helps to put difficulties into perspective, especially when individual experiences provide a good laugh.

**Preliminary meeting**

To form a study-support group all you have to do is to invite two or three others, who you think might be interested, to a preliminary meeting to discuss the formation of a group. This number is sufficient for starting, but the ideal is between six and ten, so as to have a variety of ideas, and also so as to allow for one or two absentees. At this preliminary meeting:

1. Decide on a place, a date and a time for the first meeting.
2. Ask each one to invite a friend or two along.
3. Arrange who will facilitate the meeting, who will prepare the prayer, who provide the refreshments, who will present the topic for discussion.
4. Choose a book from which to study. I recommend that new groups start with a book that deals with several subjects so as to get an overall introduction to Christian feminist thought. This

book was written for that purpose. Other books are *Women in the Church*, edited by Madonna Kolbenschlag, published (1987) by Pastoral Press, Washington DC, and distributed by Columba Book Service, 93 The Rise, Mount Merrion Avenue, Blackrock, Co. Dublin; *Womanspirit Rising*, edited by Carol P. Christ and Judith Plaskow, published (1979) by Harper, San Francisco.

5. Ask those coming to the meeting to get the book in advance and to read the first chapter. By doing this you ensure that those coming to the first meeting have some common ground on which to share and no one is left feeling 'out of it'.

6. Refreshments: Some groups decide not to have any; others prefer them at the end when those who wish to leave can and those who wish to stay on chatting have the opportunity to do so. Yet others prefer the refreshments during a break in the meeting, then during the chat ideas can be tested and the meeting has a definite ending.

### The first meeting

The first meeting will last either one and a half or two hours depending on whether refreshments are served in the middle or at the end of the meeting.

OPENING PRAYER (3-5 minutes). To focus on the fact that the group is striving to come to a fuller understanding of God.

INTRODUCTIONS Give a minute's quiet for members to consider their hopes and fears for the group, then ask them to introduce themselves and to share their thoughts.

DISCUSSION OF TOPIC The person presenting the topic now gives a summary of the chapter read, and raises one or two points (5 minutes). The floor is now open for general discussion (30 minutes).

FACILITATOR This is when the facilitating skills are required. It is important to see that each one has an opportunity to speak, and that no one member monopolises the discussion. A method I find helpful starts with a listening process. Each one in turn shares what for her was the most important idea. No one interrupts or responds until all have shared. This ensures that no one can leave the meeting saying she could not get a word in. It also provides for a pool of ideas from which to choose for the general discussion. If the method is explained beforehand it issues a warning in advance and anonymously to anyone inclined to dominate a meeting, that listening is also required. The facilitator then asks which ideas the group would like to pursue and so the general discussion begins.

REFRESHMENTS (1 hour)

CLOSING BUSINESS:

1. Ask if members are willing to commit themselves to five more meetings.
2. Decide on frequency of meetings, weekly, fortnightly, or monthly.
3. Decide date, time and venue for the next meeting. It is wiser to meet in a neutral place, or to rotate between two or three houses, so that the group is not associated with any one person. Also, remember, it may not be convenient for some members to offer their home facilities and that should be understood and accepted.
4. If it is a mixed group, ie. women and men, experience has shown that both men and women find it helpful to have some meetings with their own sex only. This has not proved divisive.
5. Arrange for a facilitator for the next meeting, for a prayer leader, a topic presenter, and a person to take care of the refreshments.

Eventually each group finds its own rhythm and focus. The 'Sophia' group to which I belong, met and studied for two years before we felt ready to undertake a group action. We chose the area of education and each year organise one or two seminars for the public. From the seminar held specifically for men there was formed a men's group. They call themselves 'Listen'.